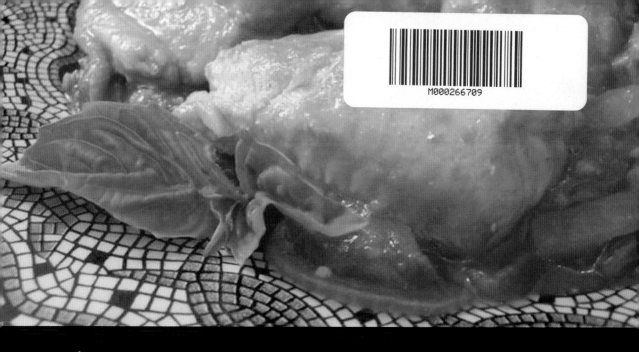

CURRY ASIA!

by Celeste Heiter

CURRY ASIA!
by Celeste Heiter

ThingsAsian Press
San Francisco, California, USA
www.thingsasianpress.com

Printed in Hong Kong

ISBN-10: 1-934159-47-6
ISBN-13: 978-1-934159-47-7

Photo Credit:
Food photos by Celeste Heiter. Others as listed: pg 20 Wet market, Hong Kong. Albert Wen; pg 24. India. Nana Chen; pg 30. Galle Fort, Sri Lanka. Albert Wen; pg 38. India. Nana Chen; pg 42. Taj Mahal, India. Albert Wen; pg 56. New Delhi, India. Albert Wen; pg 64. India. Nana Chen; pg 68. Spices. Nana Chen; pg 72. India. Nana Chen; pg 94. Kathmandu, Nepal. ©2002 Jeff Greenwald; pg 100. Mt. Kailash, Tibet. ©2002 Jeff Greenwald; pg 104. Bhutan. Kim Indresano; pg 108. Bhutan. Kim Indresano; pg 128. Fish sauce. Albert Wen; pg 130. Yangon, Myanmar. Albert Wen; pg 138. Thailand. Albert Wen; pg 140. Bangkok, Thailand. Albert Wen; pg 152. Luang Prabang, Laos. Albert Wen; pg 166. Hanoi, Vietnam. Albert Wen; pg170. Luang Prabang, Laos. Albert Wen; pg 178. Malacca, Malaysia. Albert Wen; pg 186. Singapore. Albert Wen; pg 194. Bali, Indonesia. Albert Wen; pg 212. Bali, Indonesia. Albert Wen; pg 224. Shanghai, China. Albert Wen; pg 230. Tokyo, Japan. Robert George; pg 234. Seoul, S. Korea. Albert Wen; pg 242. Tokyo, Japan. Robert George; pg 249. Spices. Albert Wen; pg 251. Curry. Albert Wen; pg 252. Spices. Albert Wen; pg 255. Spices. Albert Wen.

For Will:
my helper, shopper, taster, treasure

 Acknowledgements

With Special Thanks to:
My friend and publisher Albert Wen
My editor Janet Brown
The Safeway Delivery Team
And to my friend and neighbor Victoria Castle-Curry, for her Peacock Bowl

 Table of Contents

Foreword

I still remember the first time I tasted curry. It was the spring of 1978, at the antebellum home of an elderly, flamboyantly gay gentleman in Mobile, Alabama, my hometown. And much to my surprise, the choice of meats for his curry dish was goat!

I've always been adventurous when it comes to food, although there are a few things that I patently refuse to eat, namely: the brains, heart, tongue, liver, kidneys, tripe, or sexual organs of any animal, anything in the insect family, any endangered species, anything too slimy or stinky, and anything so risky that it may result in my untimely death. That still leaves lots of room for some interesting experiences, including cactus, seaweed, snails, squid, venison, squirrel, alligator, yak, ostrich, and yes, even goat.

On the buffet table that day, it was cooked to perfection. The meat was meltingly tender, the sauce was a lovely shade of cellophane yellow, not too mild, but not too spicy either. It was love at first bite, but it would be many years before I attempted a batch of curry in my own kitchen, and you can bet it wasn't goat.

When I lived in Tokyo, my son's father used to experiment with lots of homemade curry recipes, using a mortar and pestle to grind the spices. On occasion, we also resorted to Japanese curry mix as a quick-fix meal.

Over the years since then, I have also eaten my share of curry in Indian restaurants. My favorite is Gaylord's at Ghirardelli Square in San Francisco. The view is fantastic, and the menu features every kind of curry dish imaginable. They make a heavenly mulligatawny soup, and their puffy-golden *naan* bread looks as if it might defy gravity.

In the past fifteen years, I've made so many of pots of curry in my own kitchen that I've long since lost count. Admittedly, for the first few years, on those occasions when I made curry, I used a store-bought curry powder and simply added lots of it to a big pot of meat and vegetable stew.

Somewhere in my travels, I bought a tin of curry powder that nicely suited my tastes. The only problem was that I could no longer remember where I got it. When my stash began to run out, I decided that it was time to learn how to blend my own.

Thus began my love affair with curry. When ThingsAsian publisher Albert Wen asked what I would like the focus of my next book to be, without hesitation I answered, "*Curry Asia!*"

Introduction:
A Word that Inspired a Cuisine

Curry. The word itself conjures up a kaleidoscope of exotic aromas and fiery flavors. From the deep drama of the spices to the heady perfume of the aromatics, curry is a gustatory celebration, an infusion of history and culture. Curry is culinary creativity at its best.

Although there is much speculation among linguistic and anthropological scholars regarding the exact origins of curry, many seem to agree that the word is derived from *kari*, an ancient Tamil word that means "spiced sauce". Such a broad definition of curry offers much room for interpretation.

In today's culinary landscape, variations on the concept are common to nearly every cuisine on the planet. Curry is most closely associated with India; however, the Himalayas, Southeast Asia, Indonesia, the Middle East, West Africa, and the Caribbean islands all add their own richly varied array of dishes to the curry genre. Curry has also been assimilated into European cuisines, most notably those of England and the Netherlands, and is on the threshold of its culinary heyday in the United States.

The earliest recorded reference to curry appears in a recipe for meat cooked in a spicy sauce, etched in cuneiform on a Sumerian clay tablet circa 1700 B.C., found near ancient Babylon in what is now modern-day Iraq. Curry-like dishes were mentioned in ancient Roman records, as well as in the Sri Lankan epic poem, the *Mahavamsa*, which dates back to the 5th century. Thereafter references to curry may be found in various European literary sources, including a 16th century Dutch travel journal, the 1886 *Hobson-Jobson: Glossary of Colloquial Anglo-Indian Words and Phrases*, Alan Davidson's *Oxford Companion to Food*, a Chauceresque passage in F.J.Furnell's *Manners and Meals in Olden Times*, and William Makepeace Thackeray's poem, *Kitchen Melodies—Curry*.

The legacy of curry cookbooks includes the first English recipe collection, *The Forme of Cury*, which was commissioned by Richard II in the late 14th century. Fast-forward to 1747, when Hannah Glasse published the first known *currey* [sic] recipe in her book, *Glasse's Art of Cookery*. And in 1791, Scottish noblewoman Stephana Malcom, granddaughter of the Laird of Craig, published *In the Laird's Kitchen: Three Hundred Years of Food in Scotland*, which features a dish called "Chicken Topperfield plus Currypowder, Chutnies and Mulligatawny Soup." The 19th century *Book of Household Management* by Isabella Mary Beeton includes recipes for more than a dozen types of curry. And in his famed *Apicius Redivivus, or the Cook's Oracle*, the eccentric Dr. William Kitchiner in 1817 provided a recipe for Indian curry powder that is still in use today.

It should be noted that the use of the word curry in the English language is derived not from the Tamil *kari*, but from the French word *cuire*, which simply means *to cook*. But whether it's a matter of ancient etymology or simply a happy coincidence, both words have become synonymous with the transcendent cuisine that inspired *Curry Asia!*

How to Use and Enjoy This Book

Curry Asia! is divided into five geographic regions: The Indian Subcontinent, The Himalayas, Southeast Asia, The Islands, and The Far East. Each section focuses on the Asian countries within that region, and features one or more curry recipes from the cuisine of each country. At the end of each section, I have also included an array of side dishes to complete the meals.

The recipes I have created for *Curry Asia!* are for dishes that I believe represent the cuisine of each country or culture. Some are classics prepared according to tradition; others are my own creations, based upon my perceptions of indigenous flavors and ingredients. Global cuisine is a vibrant and evolving art that is open to as many interpretations as there are cooks and hungry diners who enjoy it. While I have tried to adhere to traditional ingredients and methods, I have also modified my recipes for ease of preparation, availability of ingredients, and my own sense of taste.

Most importantly, the dishes I've created are especially suited for entertaining. However, unless you're hosting a very large gathering with lots of help in the kitchen, I don't recommend that you try more than a few of them at once. For a party of four to six people, select three to five dishes and save the others to enjoy at another meal.

Each chapter is complemented with informative side bars; at the end of the book, you'll find a chapter titled *Resources*, which contains a list of recommended cookware and utensils, along with recipes for stocks and a basic curry powder.

Create…Cook…Capture

When it comes to recipes, I'm a *kamikaze* cook. I dive headlong into the preparation process, making things up as I go along, and I rarely follow a recipe to the letter. There are also certain foods that I can't or won't eat. I sometimes have to adjust a recipe accordingly, by either omitting or substituting certain ingredients. My inspiration for the recipes I create comes from the menagerie of cookbooks in my kitchen library and from the abundance of recipe sources on the Internet.

First, I research the cuisine of the featured country and study dozens of dishes and recipes, until I have a strong a sense of the way ingredients are combined to produce the unique flavors of each culture. Once I've decided on a dish, I gather many versions of the recipe, and as I prepare the dish, I improvise and personalize the recipe so that it becomes my own.

For my food photographs, I use a Canon Eos 1000D digital SLR camera, and I have a little photography studio set up near the windows at the far end of my kitchen. The dishes I prepare come off the stove or out of the oven and are immediately arranged on serving dishes. I photograph them *au naturale*, with no tricks or artificial visual enhancements, and no major photo editing beyond a little cropping or the occasional airbrush touch-up to remove small imperfections. Be assured that if you follow my cooking instructions, your renditions of my curry dishes will be as beautiful and delicious as those that come out of my own kitchen.

Where to Find Asian Ingredients:

Every metropolitan area will have one—if not several—or even dozens of international markets, whether specifically devoted to the kind of cuisine you're preparing, or to Asian ingredients in general. Even if you live in a small city, chances are that it will have at least one Asian market. With the growing demand for Asian ingredients, large supermarkets now carry an impressive array. If your city has an import emporium such as CostPlus World Market, they may also carry Asian ingredients. But in the event that the town where you live doesn't offer Asian ingredients locally, there's always the Internet. Here is a list of Internet sites that offer ingredients for each country:

Asian Food Shopping Websites:

Asia: EthnicFoodsCo.com, Amazon.com

Cambodia: AsianFoodGrocer.com, GroceryThai.com, ImportFood.com

China: OrientalSuper-Mart.com

Himalayas: Yakmeat.us

India: IShopIndian.com

Japan: AsianFoodGrocer.com

Korea: KoaMart.com

Philippines: Filipino-store.com

Singapore/Malaysia/Indonesia: IShopIndian.com

Thailand: ImportFood.com, GroceryThai.com

Vietnam: EthnicFoodsCo.com, Amazon.com

Cooking Notes and Tips:

Quality Ingredients: When you're making Asian cuisine at home, simple doesn't always mean quick and easy. With all the washing, cleaning, chopping, cooking, arranging, and garnishing, the preparation of many Asian dishes can be labor- intensive. And the amount of work that goes into an Asian meal is the same, whether you make it with cheap, inferior ingredients or more costly top-quality ones. Therefore, it is always important to buy the freshest and very best products you can afford, ensuring that your labor of love doesn't end up a big disappointment because you tried to cut corners. If you're going to go to all that effort, don't skimp. Buy the best!

Mise En Place: Preparing a multi-course meal for a social gathering can be complex and time consuming. However, one of the best ways to reduce the stress of getting everything off the stove and onto the table in a timely manner is the art of *mise en place*, a French term that means to prepare and set up as much of the meal ahead of time as possible. In many cases, I do all my prep the day before, and store the various components on plates or in divided storage containers overnight. Ingredients such as chopped vegetables, marinated meats, and stuffing mixtures will be fine in the refrigerator until cooking time the following day. And while I'm at it, I also get out all my utensils, cooking vessels, and tableware, so all that's left to do on the day of the dinner is to fire it up!

Esoteric Ingredients: Most authentic curry recipes contain an esoteric ingredient, if not several. Unfortunately, such rarities are not always available at the corner grocery market. In most cases, I suggest more commonly available substitutes that produce a similar taste.

Among those most commonly called for are fresh curry leaves, kaffir lime leaves, and two ginger-like roots: galangal, and *krachai*. Those who live in or near large cities may find these aromatics in the fresh produce sections of Asian markets, and they may also be found at upscale markets in certain areas.

Fresh gingerroot may be substituted for galangal and krachai;, however, there is no substitute for fresh curry leaves and kaffir lime leaves. Given their hit-or-miss availability, in my recipes, I have either designated them as "optional," or left them out altogether. But the unique flavor that they add to a curry dish makes it worthwhile to seek out a local source for them.

Another somewhat esoteric ingredient, especially in Indonesian curries, is *terasi*, an intensely flavorful, fermented shrimp paste. And although I recognize the importance of adding it to certain curry pastes for authenticity's sake, I don't enjoy the funky aftertaste it leaves behind. So as a matter of personal preference, I don't typically include terasi in my recipes.

Salt and Pepper: Unlike many Western cuisines, Asian food does not automatically include the addition of salt and pepper. Individual sensitivities and restricted diets vary, so, if at all, I usually list "salt and pepper to taste." Many Asian dishes contain spicy chili peppers, so the addition of black pepper is not necessary, and sauces and condiments such as soy sauce and Asian fish sauce are extremely salty. As an eye-opening experiment to illustrate just how salty they are, pour a little soy sauce or fish sauce in a shallow saucer and leave it out overnight. You will be amazed at the salt crystals that form as the liquid evaporates.

Cooking Oils: Each Asian cuisine favors certain types of cooking oils, including olive, peanut, sesame, mustard, and the buttery-golden ghee used in Indian recipes; and each oil brings its own unique flavor to a dish. Olive oil is rich and subtle, while sesame and mustard oils are quite strong and should be used sparingly. Melted butter may be used instead of ghee, but there is really no substitute for its deep, nutty flavor. It's worth the extra effort to make it yourself if it's not commercially available. Generally speaking, I use these flavored oils for stir-frying, dips, and dressings. And for deep-frying, I use generic vegetable oil because it is economically priced and does not impart a strong flavor to fried foods.

While I'm on the subject, it's always best to use fresh oil that hasn't been previously used for frying other foods, and don't overcrowd your wok or pan. Be sure to leave plenty of room for turning foods in a bubbly frying pan, and for tossing the ingredients in a busy stir-fry.

Stocks and Broth: Many of my recipes call for stock or broth. Although high-quality commercially prepared stocks are readily available and perfectly fine to use, I prefer to make my own. It's a great way to reduce kitchen waste (bones and skin, vegetable trimmings, etc.) I make it in large batches and store it in the freezer for convenience. This is time consuming, so be sure to allow a couple of extra hours for making homemade stock. Basic stock recipes are included in the Resources chapter at the end of the book.

Chicken: The various cuts of chicken have different flavors and textures. For flavor, I prefer thighs; however, the boneless thigh meat is not always as tender and uniformly attractive as breasts. So I recommend thighs for some recipes, and breasts for others, but you may use whichever you prefer.

Beef, Lamb, and Pork: Religion plays a significant role in the types of meats consumed in each country's cuisine. The Muslim faith prohibits the consumption of pork, beef is not commonly eaten by Hindus, and many Buddhists avoid meat altogether. In this collection of recipes, I have tried to remain mindful of these various religious preferences, and therefore do not recommend certain meats in recipes from cultures where they might be restricted.

Rice and Noodles: The recipes in this collection call for several different types of rice, including jasmine, basmati, brown, wild, and medium- or short-grain rice. However, unless otherwise specified, the standard for a recipe that simply calls for "rice" is long-grain white rice. My favorite choice for white rice is to mix equal parts long-grain and medium-grain rice. This combination yields a slightly sticky texture that holds up well with sauces, and for eating plain, whether scooped by hand, with flatbread, or with chopsticks. Regarding noodles, the recipes in this collection generally call for long strands of commercially produced dry pasta.

Garlic, Ginger, and Chili Peppers: I love all three, so I like to add lots of these aromatic ingredients to recipes that call for them. In general, my recipes indicate "cloves of garlic," "knob of gingerroot," and in some cases, "whole chili peppers." But you may adjust the amounts to suit your individual tastes. Most of my recipes call for jalapeño peppers with the seeds and membranes removed. Although I love the taste of chilies, I have a sensitive palate, so, except in rare instances, I typically avoid the high-end varieties such as Thai and habanero. Feel free to use them if you dare, but be sure to wear protective gloves when handling chilies.

My favorite way to add the flavor of chilies is to use the only pods of green or red jalapeños with the seeds removed, and add dried red chili flakes according to my own taste. This way I get the fresh taste of the chili peppers, but I can control how hot the finished dish will be with the addition of dried red chili flakes.

Chili Sauces and Pastes: The cuisines of Asia feature a seemingly endless variety of chili-based condiments, including Chinese chili oil and chili-garlic sauce, Southeast Asian *sriracha*, and Indonesian *sambal oelek*, to name a few. There are subtle differences in flavor and intensity, but for the most part, you may use them interchangeably according to your tastes.

Spotlight on Spice: The Scoville Scale for Chili Peppers

The Scoville Scale is a graduated chart that lists chili peppers according to their capsaicin content, which determines the degree of peppery heat. Pimentos and bell peppers of any color have a zero value on the Scoville scale. Cherry peppers and Italian pepperoncini register up to 500 units, followed by El Paso, Santa Fe Grande, and Coronado at up to 1,000.

Espanola, poblano, ancho, mulato, pasilla, anaheim, sandia, numex, and rocotillo varieties register up to 2,500 units. Mirasol and guajillo come in at up to 5,000 units, while chipotle and other jalapeños are up to 8,000. Hot wax peppers and puya may reach 10,000.

The 17,000 to 30,000 range includes hidalgo, Serrano, manzano, shipkas, and de arbol varieties. Levels of capsaicin up to 50,000 units may be found in jaloro, aji, Tabasco, cayenne, santaka and piquin. In the 75,000 to 100,000 unit range there are yatsafusa, haimen, chiltecpin and Thai. The *capsicum annuum* variety used in Himalayan cuisine register 50,000 to 100,000.

Things really heat up in the 110,000 to 225,000 unit range with tabiche, Bahamian, Carolina cayenne, kumataka, Jamaican hot, and bird's eye. Near the top of the chart, habanero and Scotch bonnet measure up to 325,000 units. The red savina habanero variety tops the scale with a whopping 577,000 units at maximum strength.

Curry Asia!

The Indian Subcontinent

This flavorful culinary journey through Asia begins on the Indian subcontinent, which includes India, Sri Lanka, Pakistan and Bangladesh. India itself is also divided into twenty-eight states and seven union territories. For the purposes of this book, I have divided the Indian subcontinent into four geographic regions: South, Central, North, and East. I start in the state of Tamil Nadu, where it is believed that curry originated. From there, I wind my way through Sri Lanka and South India, onward through the vast central region, then north through Pakistan, North India, East India, and finally, into Bangladesh. While no cookbook could possibly encompass the entirety of its curries, I'd like to think that I have represented the Indian subcontinent with an enticing array of its best curry dishes.

Tamil Nadu: Where It All Began

With the etymological origins of the word *curry* in the Tamil language, and perhaps even the origins of curry itself, I thought, "What better place to embark upon my journey?"

Tamil cuisine in general, and Tamil curry in particular, are characterized by an intoxicating array of aromatic spices, including cumin, coriander, cinnamon, cloves, cardamom, nutmeg, mustard, fennel, and black peppercorns. The flavors of Tamil curry are further enhanced by the addition of ginger, garlic, onions, chilies, curry leaves, and coconut.

For religious reasons, a significant demographic within the Tamil diet features a variety of vegetarian dishes made with rice, legumes, lentils, garden vegetables, and dairy products. However, given its proximity to the coastal waters of the Gulf of Mannar, the Bay of Bengal, and the Indian Ocean, seafood is also a prominent main ingredient among the non-vegetarian population.

For my Tamil curry, I have created an enticing seafood dish. I chose *basa*, a Southeast Asian catfish, for its firm texture and sweet flavor. However, nearly any seafood could be used as the main ingredient. The sauce features a classic dry-roasted *charakku* spice blend, and an infusion of basic aromatics for the curry paste, with coconut milk for the broth. The result is a transcendent gestalt of sweet, savory, and spicy that complements the fish with subtlety and finesse. This is a truly elegant curry.

Tamil Fish Curry

Serves 4

Charakku Spice Blend:
1 tablespoon cumin seeds
1 tablespoon coriander seeds
1 tablespoon yellow mustard seeds
1 tablespoon fennel seeds
1/2 teaspoon black peppercorns

Curry Paste:
1 large shallot, peeled and coarsely chopped
1 green jalapeño pepper, seeded and coarsely chopped
4 cloves garlic, peeled and coarsely chopped
Charakku spice blend (see recipe)
1 teaspoon turmeric
1 teaspoon paprika
1 lime, juice only
1/4 cup water (as needed)

Tamil Fish Curry:
3 fresh curry leaves (optional)
Curry paste (see recipe)
1 can unsweetened coconut milk (13.5 ounces)
1 tablespoon peanut oil
1 pound firm white fish, cut into large chunks
Salt to taste

Charakku Spice Blend:
Dry-roast whole seeds in a skillet over low heat until fragrant and lightly browned. Set aside to cool. Grind roasted seeds to a fine powder with a mortar and pestle, or with an electric spice grinder. Set aside until needed.

Curry Paste:
Place all ingredients except water in a blender or food processor. Puree mixture to a fine paste, adding water a little at a time as needed for consistency. Set aside until needed.

Tamil Fish Curry:

If using curry leaves, toast them in a small skillet over medium heat until fragrant. Bring curry paste to a simmer in a small saucepan. Add curry leaves if using, reduce heat, cover, and continue simmering for 5 minutes, stirring frequently. Stir in coconut milk and continue simmering uncovered for 15 minutes, until sauce is thickened. While curry sauce is simmering, heat oil in a skillet. Add fish and pan-fry over medium heat, turning occasionally, until pieces are fully cooked and lightly browned on both sides. Spoon about 1/4 cup of curry sauce into shallow bowls. Place fish on top and drizzle with remaining sauce. Serve with steamed rice or flatbread. (Sounds so good! I've never toasted curry leaves—have to try!)

Spotlight on Spice: Curry Leaves

The curry tree is a tropical species that is indigenous to Asia and the Indian subcontinent. Its species name *Murraya koenigii*, is an homage to German botanist and physician Johann Köenig, whose scientific studies in Asia with the British East India Company earned him a footnote in botanical history.

The curry tree grows to a height of twelve to twenty feet tall, with aromatic leaves that are valued for their flavor and medicinal properties. The curry tree also produces clusters of small, fragrant white flowers and small berry-like fruit that turns from red to black when ripe.

As with the savory dishes that share its name, the term "curry" comes from the Tamil language. Known in Tamil Nadu as *kariveppilai*, its name means "curry neem leaf", and is widely used in Tamil-style curry dishes, as well as in curries throughout India and Southeast Asia. Sometimes called "sweet neem leaf", curry leaves are typically added in the initial phase of cooking, along with onions, garlic, and ginger. Curry leaves are best when fresh, although they may also be dried, but with a significant loss of flavor and aroma.

Curry Asia!

Sri Lanka

At only 25,332 square miles, this teardrop of an island just off the southern tip of India features remarkable culinary diversity. Hill- country cuisine is quite different from that of the coastal regions, and with its proximity to the mainland state of Tamil Nadu, much of Sri Lanka's population is of Tamil heritage.

In addition to its regional fare, in common with many Asian cuisines, Sri Lankan cuisine is an amalgam of dishes influenced over centuries by many cultures, including Indian, Middle-Eastern, Malaysian, Portuguese, Dutch, and British. Predictably, many of the dishes introduced by these traders and invaders have been adapted to Sri Lanka's culinary ethos by the use of local ingredients.

Among them are tropical fruits such as coconut, pineapple, papaya, melon, passion fruit, and guava; plantains, bananas, and mangoes in many shapes and sizes; and the more exotic cashew apple, durian, mangosteen, wood apple, and rambutan. Vegetables come in two categories: hill- country varieties such as cabbage, carrot, beetroot, cauliflower, kohlrabi, beans, tomatoes, and bell peppers; and low country vegetables such as leafy greens, eggplant, cucumber, pumpkin, bitter gourd, loofah gourd, and snake gourd. Spices and other flavoring agents include chili peppers, ginger, garlic, turmeric, mustard seeds, cumin, coriander, cardamom, clove, nutmeg, mace, and cinnamon.

In this island cuisine, seafood is naturally a prime ingredient, including prawns, crabs, lobsters, tuna, mullet, and squid. In addition to the essential place of seafood as a fresh ingredient, pickled and dried fish are also common in many Sri Lankan dishes. As with every cuisine, its dishes vary with each individual who prepares them. Every family has its own style and preferences, with each day's fare being improvisational, according to the season. Cooks tend to rely on instinct and taste, rather than precise recipes.

Sri Lankan curry runs the gamut, from meat, seafood, and vegetables to fruit and spices, and may be served for breakfast, lunch, or dinner. A typical non-vegetarian curry includes some kind of protein (meat or seafood), two or more vegetables, a variety of spices including chili peppers, cinnamon, cardamom, cloves, and nutmeg, with coconut milk as the most common liquid ingredient.

A typical Sri Lankan meal might include both a 'main curry' of meat or fish, and one or more vegetable or legume curries. Sri Lankan curries tend to be fiery hot, and are served with an accompaniment of even more fiery *sambals*, piquant chutneys and pickles, cooling salads, plain rice, and a lentil flatbread called *pappadum*. At a Sri Lankan curry meal, everything is served at once. The rice is hand-scooped in bite-sized morsels, with a bit of this-and-that from the other dishes in each bite.

Curry Asia!

Sri Lankan Vinegar Shrimp

Serves 4

Curry Paste:

4 cloves garlic, peeled and coarsely chopped
1 shallot, peeled and coarsely chopped
1 knob gingerroot, peeled and coarsely chopped (about 1 tablespoon)
1 jalapeño pepper, seeded and coarsely chopped
1 teaspoon turmeric
1/4 teaspoon cayenne pepper (more or less to taste)
1/4 cup water (as needed)

Sri Lankan Vinegar Shrimp:

24 large shrimp, peeled and deveined, tails intact
1 teaspoon yellow mustard seeds
Curry paste (see recipe)
2 tablespoons peanut oil
3 fresh curry leaves (optional)
2 jalapeño peppers, seeded and thinly sliced
1/4 cup coconut vinegar (substitute sugarcane, rice, or apple cider vinegar)
Salt to taste

Curry Paste:

Place all ingredients except water in a blender or food processor. Puree mixture to a fine paste, adding water a little at a time as needed for consistency. Set aside until needed.

Sri Lankan Vinegar Shrimp:

In a large bowl, combine shrimp, mustard seeds and curry paste. Stir gently to evenly coat the shrimp. Marinate for 1 hour. Heat the oil in a large skillet, add curry leaves if using, and quickly stir-fry until fragrant. Add marinated shrimp and stir-fry until they turn pink, about 3 minutes. Add vinegar, jalapeño, and salt. Reduce heat and simmer for about 3 minutes, until peppers are tender.

Sri Lankan Curry Pork Ribs

Serves 4

Sri Lankan Curry Powder:
1 teaspoon cumin seeds
1 teaspoon coriander seeds
1 teaspoon fennel seeds
1/2 teaspoon fenugreek seeds
1/2 cinnamon stick, coarsely crushed
6 green cardamom pods
6 cloves
3 curry leaves

Curry Paste:
1 onion, peeled and coarsely chopped
6 cloves garlic, peeled and coarsely chopped
1 knob gingerroot, peeled and coarsely chopped (about 1 tablespoon)
1 jalapeño pepper, seeded and coarsely chopped
1 tablespoon Sri Lankan curry powder (see recipe)
1 teaspoon turmeric
1/4 teaspoon cayenne pepper (more or less to taste)
1/4 cup water (as needed)

Braising the Ribs:
2 pork rib racks, 2 to 3 pounds each, cut into 8-inch segments

Barbeque Sauce:
1 can diced tomatoes, with juice (14.5 ounces)
Curry paste (see recipe above)
1 cup pork broth (reserved from braised ribs)
1/4 cup brown sugar
Salt to taste

Sri Lankan Curry Powder:

Combine all ingredients in a heavy skillet and place over low heat, gently shaking the pan until the spices are fragrant and lightly toasted. Remove from the heat and set aside to cool. Transfer toasted spices to an electric grinder, blender, or stone mortar and grind to a fine powder. Set aside until needed.

Cook's Note: Leftover curry powder may be stored in an airtight jar for later use.

Curry Paste:

Place all ingredients except water in a blender or food processor. Puree mixture to a fine paste, adding water a little at a time as needed for consistency. Set aside until needed.

Braising the Ribs:

Fill a large, deep kettle with water and bring to a boil. Add ribs, reduce heat and simmer for one hour. Remove ribs from water and transfer to a foil-lined baking sheet. Cover and set aside. Reserve 1 cup of pork broth for making the sauce.

Cook's Note: The remaining pork broth may be refrigerated or frozen for later use.

Barbeque Sauce:

Combine all ingredients in a saucepan and bring to a simmer. Reduce heat, and continue simmering, stirring occasionally, for about 45 minutes, until sauce is thickened. Remove from heat, and set aside to cool. Transfer to a blender or food processor and puree to a fine consistency. Transfer to a bowl and set aside until time to cook the ribs.

Finishing the Ribs:

Preheat oven to 275 degrees. Brush both sides of ribs with barbeque sauce and place on the middle rack of the oven. Bake ribs for about 1 hour, turning and basting with sauce every 15 minutes. Remove from the oven and serve immediately.

Cook's Note: Ribs may also be grilled on a well-oiled stovetop grill pan or an outdoor barbeque.

South India

For the purposes of my culinary itinerary, I have designated South India as the states of Goa, Karnataka, Andhra Pradesh, Yanam, Kerala, Mahe, Pondicherry, Karaikal, and Tamil Nadu. This region features a lengthy coastline that runs along the Arabian Sea to the west, the Indian Ocean to the south, and the Bay of Bengal to the east.

The coastlines are fringed with sandy beaches. Farther inland, the deeply forested Eastern and Western Coastal Plains are traversed by a network of rivers flowing into deltas that empty into the surrounding waters. The climate of South India is rainy and humid, with a summer monsoon season that feeds the river systems.

The flood plains of South India yield an abundance of rice, lentils, and other agricultural products to feed a largely vegetarian population. However, South Indian cuisine is also characterized by its use of seafood and tropical fruit.

Curry is a way of life in South India. With its varied religious population, meats, seafood, and an abundant array of vegetables are all used as main ingredients. Ablaze with fiery chili peppers, South Indian curries also feature an exotic array of spices, including cumin, coriander, turmeric, mustard seeds, cardamom, cloves, cinnamon, and black pepper. Coconut milk is a common component in many South Indian curry dishes. Rice, lentils, and flatbreads are served as accompaniments, along with tropical fruit pickles and chutneys.

For my South Indian curry dish, I've chosen to focus on the Goa region, which was once under Portuguese colonial rule. Goa is famed for its *vindaloo*, a Portuguese inspired curry that was originally made with *vin d'ail*, the preserved meats brought over by Portuguese traders in barrels of garlic-laced wine. The flavorful ingredient list for *vindaloo* includes ginger, garlic, red wine vinegar, mustard, onions, cumin, coriander, turmeric, and dried chilies.

Pork Vindaloo

Serves 4

Vindaloo Paste:

Whole Spices:
1 teaspoon cumin seeds
1 teaspoon coriander seeds
1 teaspoon mustard seeds
6 whole cloves
10 black peppercorns

Powdered Spices:
1 teaspoon turmeric
1 teaspoon paprika
1/2 teaspoon cinnamon
1/2 teaspoon dried chili flakes

Fresh Ingredients:
12 cloves garlic, peeled and coarsely chopped
1 large knob of gingerroot, peeled and coarsely chopped
1 shallot, peeled and coarsely chopped
1/3 cup red wine vinegar
1/4 cup peanut oil

Pork Vindaloo:
2 pounds boneless pork, cut into bite-sized pieces
Vindaloo paste (see recipe)
1 tablespoon peanut oil
1 small onion, peeled and thinly sliced
2 jalapeño peppers, seeded and thinly sliced
4 cups water

Vindaloo Paste:
Place whole spices in a spice grinder or stone mortar and grind to a fine powder. Combine with powdered spices and fresh ingredients in a food processor and puree to a fine paste. Set aside until needed.

Pork Vindaloo:

To Marinate: Combine pork and vindaloo paste in a large glass bowl and stir thoroughly. Cover and place in the refrigerator to marinate for four hours, or overnight.

To Prepare: Heat peanut oil in a large kettle or skillet. Add onions and stir-fry until translucent and tender. Add marinated pork and the remainder of the vindaloo paste and continue stir-frying until pork is lightly browned. Add water and bring to a simmer. Reduce heat and continue simmering until pork is tender and sauce is thickened, about 45 minutes. In the last 5 minutes of cooking time, add jalapeño peppers and continue simmering until peppers are just tender. Serve with steamed rice and flatbread.

Central India

For my culinary journey through India, I have designated the central region as the states of Rajasthan, Uttar Pradesh, Bihar, Jharkhand, Madhya Pradesh, Gujarat, Dadra and Nagar Haveli, Maharashtra, Chhattisgarh, and Orissa.

The geography of central India varies widely, from its steep mountain peaks, to the valleys carved by the rivers that flow out of them. The flood plains below include those created by the Ganges and Indus rivers. Central India also includes the Eastern and Western Coastal Plains. These fertile regions are ideal for the cultivation of rice, wheat, corn, sugarcane, and cotton.

Central India cuts a broad swath across the subcontinent, and within it, there is a kaleidoscope of culinary styles and flavors. Cuisine runs the gamut from the hearty curries of Rajasthan, rich with dairy products and earthy spices, to the light-yet-fiery Maharashtra-style curries; and coastal cuisine, with its bounty of seafood, laden with the tropical flavors of kaffir lime and coconut milk. To represent Central India, I have created a dry, tandoori-style chicken, and a festive rice biryani.

Tandoori cuisine refers to the *tandoor*, a huge, fiery-hot clay oven used to cook tandoori dishes. Although most home kitchens cannot accommodate such an imposing cooking device, a close approximation may be achieved in a standard oven set at the highest temperature.

Most tandoori recipes start with a yogurt and lemon juice base for the marinade, with spices added for flavor and color, including turmeric, cumin, coriander, paprika, chili powder, cayenne pepper, garam masala, garlic, and ginger. Food coloring is often added to the marinade to give the finished dish its brilliant red hue. Chicken, lamb, or even fish may be used as the main ingredient. After marinating for several hours, the meat or fish is dry-roasted to a deep, ruddy char.

Biryani is a savory rice casserole common to cuisines throughout Asia and the Middle East. The dish originated in ancient Persia It was later introduced to Asia and the subcontinent by traders along the Silk Road.

Similar to the rice medleys known as pilaf or *pilau*, biryani is distinguished by the way the dish is assembled. The main components of biryani include fragrant basmati rice, richly curried meat, seafood, or vegetables, and an array of aromatic spices such as cumin, coriander, turmeric, cinnamon, cardamom, cloves, and bay leaves. The rice is par-cooked separately; the various components are then layered in a casserole dish and baked to form a crispy rice crust on the bottom.

The dish may be made with any type of meat or seafood, and the flavor palette varies from one culture or region to the next. In addition to its popularity in the Middle East and the Indian subcontinent, biryani is common to Thailand, Myanmar, Malaysia, and the Philippines. It may be served as everyday fare in many restaurants and households; however, it is also regarded as a festive dish for special occasions such as weddings and celebratory holidays.

Tandoori-Style Chicken Wings

Serves 4

18 chicken wings, cut into segments (skin optional)
1 1/2 cups plain yogurt
1 lemon, juice only
1 knob gingerroot, peeled and finely shredded (about 1 tablespoon)

1 tablespoon curry powder
1 tablespoon paprika
1 tablespoon garlic powder
1/4 teaspoon cayenne pepper
1/4 teaspoon cinnamon
1 teaspoon red food coloring (optional)

In a large mixing bowl, combine the yogurt and lemon juice with the ginger and spices (and food coloring if using) and stir thoroughly. Add chicken wings and stir to evenly coat with yogurt mixture. Cover and marinate in the refrigerator for 4 hours, or overnight.

Preheat oven to 550 degrees. Arrange the chicken wings on a wire rack over a foil-lined baking sheet and bake until the chicken is lightly charred, about 30 minutes, turning once after 15 minutes.

Cook's Note: Chicken may also be grilled on an outdoor barbeque.

Curry Chicken Biryani

Serves 4

Curry Paste:
1 shallot, peeled and coarsely chopped
4 cloves garlic, peeled and coarsely chopped
1 jalapeño pepper, seeded and coarsely chopped
1 teaspoon cumin
1 teaspoon coriander
1 teaspoon paprika
1 teaspoon turmeric
1 teaspoon dried red chili flakes
1 large tomato, cored and coarsely chopped

Curry Filling:
2 tablespoons peanut oil
2 boneless, skinless chicken breasts, cut into small bite-sized pieces
1 small onion, peeled, halved and thinly sliced
Curry paste (see recipe)
Salt to taste

Rice:
2 tablespoons peanut oil
2 cups basmati rice
1 small onion, peeled and diced
1 teaspoon fennel seeds
2 cups chicken stock

Assembling the Biryani:
Cooking oil or spray
Par-cooked Rice
Curry Filling
2 cinnamon sticks, broken in half
4 bay leaves

Curry Paste:
Combine all ingredients in a blender or food processor and puree to a fine consistency. Set aside until needed.

Curry Filling:
Heat oil in a large skillet or wok. Add chicken and onion and stir-fry until chicken is lightly browned and onions are translucent. Stir in curry paste, reduce heat, cover and simmer for 10 minutes, stirring occasionally. Remove from heat and set aside until needed.

Rice:

Heat oil in a large saucepan. Add rice, onion and fennel seeds and stir-fry until onion is translucent and rice begins to turn opaque. Add chicken stock and bring to a simmer. Reduce heat, cover and continue simmering for 10 minutes, until liquid is absorbed. Remove from heat.

Assembling the Biryani:

Preheat oven to 300 degrees. Transfer half of the cooked rice to a lightly-oiled casserole dish with a tight-fitting lid. Spread the rice across the bottom of the dish. Add a layer of the curry filling and spread the remaining rice in an even layer over the top. Arrange bay leaves and cinnamon sticks on top of rice. Cover and bake for one hour. Remove from the oven and serve immediately.

Cook's Note: Biryani may be served in the casserole dish, or it may be transferred to a serving plate by inverting the plate over the casserole dish and turning it upside down, which will expose the crispy-brown underside of the rice.

Spotlight on Spice: Turmeric

Turmeric is an essential spice for nearly every Asian cuisine. The brilliant yellow powder originates in the fibrous networks of a rhizome in the ginger family. Native to southern Asia, turmeric thrives in tropical climates with abundant rainfall. Most of the world's turmeric is produced in the town of Sangli, in Maharashtra, India.

Known also as *kunyit*, *besar*, *haldi* or *pasupu*, the fibrous bulbs of the turmeric plant, which are similar in appearance to gingerroot, are boiled, dried, and ground into a fine powder. Ground turmeric is one of the main elements in curry powders. It may be used by itself as a mild flavoring agent, and to add its distinctive yellow color to sauces and rice dishes. Turmeric is widely used as a coloring agent in commercially prepared foods.

Turmeric is also believed to have powerful medicinal properties. It is used as an antiseptic, a pain reliever, a digestive, and is even undergoing research as a cancer-fighting agent and a treatment for Alzheimer's disease.

Pakistan

Located in South Asia, Pakistan is bordered by Afghanistan and Iran to the west, by China to the north, and by India to the east. The landscape varies widely from K2, the world's second highest mountain peak, to the tropical coastline along the Arabian Sea. The Indus River basin, one of the world's largest, is actually a network of waterways, and the vast floodplains created by this river system feature some of the world's most fertile farmland.

Pakistani cuisine is a rich and flavorful fusion, with strong influences from both India and the Middle East. Culinary styles vary from region to region, especially with regard to Sindh and Punjab, where flavors and techniques strongly resemble those of North India; and in the western provinces of Khyber Pakhtunkhwa, Balochistan, Gilgit-Baltistan and Azad Kashmir, where distinctive Afghani influences are prevalent.

Muslim dietary laws known as *halal* are strictly followed by many Pakistani people, which means abstinence from alcohol and certain types of meat, especially pork. However, the Pakistani Muslim diet does include lamb, beef, chicken, dairy, and an abundance of fruit and vegetables. Seafood is a common component in the coastal cuisines of Sindh and Makran. Curried vegetables and legumes are widely consumed, especially among the vegetarian population. Rice dishes such as *basmati pulao* and biryani, along with an enticing variety of flatbreads, are also important components of daily fare.

Pakistani cuisine is known for its rich flavors and, in certain regions, the abundant use of oil in the cooking process. Grilling and tandoori oven roasting are popular cooking methods for meat and bread, along with braising and stewing for the preparation of rich curry sauces.

Fragrant spices that lend their aromas and flavors to Pakistani cuisine include cumin, coriander, cardamom, cinnamon, cloves, nutmeg, and mace. Spice blends known as *garam masala* are also used to flavor many dishes.

As with Indian curries, the curries of Pakistan may be prepared using a dry spice rub or a spiced marinade for grilled or tandoori kebabs, or with a richly flavorful sauce made with a variety of fresh ingredients such as tomatoes, potatoes, leafy herbs, garlic, and yogurt.

Karahi (spicy grilled lamb or chicken) is one of Pakistan's most popular dishes, as is *nihari* (a rich beef or lamb shank stew), and *haleem* (a hearty Persian-style ragout of beef, wheat and lentils). *Aloo gosht* (a spicy meat and potato curry) is common fare, especially in Pakistani home kitchens.

For my Pakistani curry, I have chosen *korma*, a fragrant stew that I've made on many occasions. Here I have created a traditional version made with lamb and yogurt.

Pakistani Lamb Korma

Serves 4

Whole Spices:
1/2 stick cinnamon, coarsely crushed
6 cardamom pods
10 black peppercorns
3 whole cloves
1 teaspoon cumin seeds
1 teaspoon coriander seeds
1 bay leaf
1/2 teaspoon dried chili flakes

Korma Spice Paste:
1 small onion, peeled and coarsely chopped
1 knob gingerroot, peeled and coarsely chopped
4 cloves garlic, peeled and trimmed
1/4 cup almonds
1 teaspoon turmeric
1 teaspoon paprika
Whole spice powder (see recipe)
1/4 cup water (as needed)

Main Ingredients:
Korma spice paste (see recipe)
2 cups plain yogurt
2 pounds boneless lamb, cut into bite-sized pieces
1 tablespoon ghee (substitute butter)
4 cups lamb stock (substitute beef or chicken)
2 lemons, cut into wedges

Whole Spices:

Combine whole spices in a small skillet over medium heat and toast until fragrant and lightly browned. Set aside to cool. Transfer to a spice grinder, blender, or stone mortar and grind to a fine powder.

Combine spice paste and yogurt in a large glass bowl and stir thoroughly. Add lamb and stir gently to coat. Cover and refrigerate for 4 hours, or overnight.

Korma Spice Paste:

Place all ingredients except water in a blender or food processor. Puree mixture to a fine paste, adding water a little at a time as needed for consistency. Set aside until needed.

To Prepare Korma:

Heat ghee or butter in a stew pot or deep skillet. Transfer lamb pieces to the stew pot and save excess marinade for the sauce. Stir-fry lamb until lightly browned, add lamb stock, and bring to a simmer. Reduce heat and simmer uncovered for about 40 minutes. Add remaining marinade and continue simmering for about 20 minutes, until lamb is tender and sauce is thickened. Serve with lemon wedges, steamed rice, and flatbread.

North India

The geographic region of the Indian Subcontinent that I've designated as North India plunges deep into the continent of Asia and includes the states of Jammu and Kashmir, Himachal Pradesh, Punjab, Uttaranchal, and Haryana. North India is bordered to the west by Pakistan, to the northeast by China, and to the west by Nepal. The northern-most section is traversed by the Himalayas, and to the south is the fertile belt of land known as the Indo-Gangetic Plain.

In a region that occupies only five of India's twenty-eight states, and only about 20% of India's geography, North Indian cuisine is remarkably varied in its style and origins. Hindu, Buddhist, and Muslim influences are strong, and the fourteenth-century invasion of the conqueror Timur brought the flavors of Central Asia and Persia.

For main ingredients, lamb and mutton are favored by the Muslim population; and in the cattle-producing regions, dairy products such as yogurt, curds, butter, and a cheese called paneer are also integral to North Indian curry. Agriculture produces wheat, rice, and a millet-like grain called madua. Aromatics such as onions, garlic, and ginger are also cultivated, along with lentils and leafy greens. In addition to the meat and vegetable ingredients, spice blends known as masala are used to enhance the flavor of North Indian curries.

With its varied population, both meat and vegetarian curries are common. Daily fare in North India may range from a simple meal of curried lentils with rice and flatbread to an elaborate Pandit feast. In addition to meals prepared in home kitchens, street vendors called dhabas feed much of North India's population.

When I began researching North Indian curry, I was overwhelmed by the variety of culinary styles and cultural influences. However, as my understanding of the region came into focus, winnowing down the kaleidoscope of possibilities to one or two curry dishes was suddenly easy. There was no question that the main ingredient for one of

them would be lamb, as all my research sources named lamb as the hands-down favorite among North India's many regional cuisines. Since dairy products are so common to the region, the recipe would definitely include yogurt and ghee. Given the narrow field of agricultural produce, the other ingredients would be simple: ginger, garlic, and onions.

Within these parameters, one dish rose to the top of the list: Rogan Josh, considered by many to be North India's most popular dish. This Kashmiri curry is a lamb stew in a spicy red sauce. There are many variations on the classic Mughal dish. In addition to lamb as the main ingredient, some recipes may include yogurt, onions, tomatoes, and ground almonds. The red curry sauce gets its color from dried Kashmiri peppers, and a rich palette of both whole and ground spices creates its complex flavors.

It also occurred to me that no curry cookbook would be complete without a recipe for Chicken Masala, and it just so happens that one of my favorite masala recipes comes from the North Indian state of Bihar. Located in northeastern India near the Nepal border, Bihar is noteworthy for Mahabodhi Temple in the town of Bodhgaya, the renowned site of the Bodhi Tree where Buddha attained enlightenment.

Kashmiri Rogan Josh

Serves 4

Curry paste:
8 cloves garlic, peeled and coarsely chopped
1 knob gingerroot, peeled and coarsely chopped (about 1 tablespoon)
1 teaspoon cumin
1 teaspoon coriander
1/4 cup water (as needed)

Whole Spices:
1 cinnamon stick
2 bay leaves
6 whole cloves
6 cardamom pods
10 black peppercorns
3 dried Kashmiri chilies, crushed*

Main Ingredients:
2 tablespoons ghee (substitute clarified butter)
Whole Spices (see recipe)
2 pounds boneless lamb, cut into bite-sized pieces
1 large onion, peeled, halved and thinly sliced
Curry paste (see recipe)
1 cup plain yogurt
2 cups lamb stock (substitute water)
1 teaspoon garam masala

Curry paste:

Place all ingredients except water in a blender or food processor. Puree mixture to a fine paste, adding water a little at a time as needed for consistency. Set aside until needed.

Whole Spices:

Gather whole spices and have them standing ready to brown when starting the curry.

Cook's Note: If Kashmiri chilies are unavailable, substitute 2 teaspoons Indian paprika and a teaspoon of dried red chili flakes, and add to the curry pot with ground spices instead of browning with the whole spices. For the convenience of your dinner guests, whole spices may be removed from the sauce before serving.

Main Ingredients:

Heat ghee in a large wok or kettle with a tight-fitting lid. Add whole spices and stir-fry until fragrant and lightly browned, about 1 minute. Add lamb and onions and continue stir-frying until meat is lightly browned and onions are tender and translucent. Stir in curry paste (add paprika if using). Stir in yogurt a little at a time, add lamb stock and bring to a simmer. Cover and reduce heat. Continue simmering for about 40 minutes, until lamb is tender. Remove the lid and continue simmering until sauce is slightly thickened, about 20 minutes. Season with *garam masala*. Serve with steamed rice and flatbread.

Curry Asia!

Bihari Chicken Masala

Serves 4

Curry Paste:
4 cloves garlic, peeled and coarsely chopped
1 knob gingerroot, peeled and coarsely chopped (about 1 tablespoon)
1 shallot, peeled and coarsely chopped
1 jalapeño pepper, seeded and coarsely chopped
1/4 cup water (as needed)

Chicken:
1 tablespoon mustard oil
1 tablespoon peanut oil
2 pounds boneless chicken breasts or thighs, cut into 1-inch strips
1 large shallot, peeled and thinly sliced
Curry paste (see recipe)
2 large tomatoes, cored and coarsely chopped
1-1/2 cups chicken stock
1 teaspoon garam masala
Salt to taste
Cayenne pepper to taste
2 jalapeño peppers, seeded and thinly sliced
1/2 stick butter, cut into 4 pats

Curry Paste:
Place all ingredients except water in a blender or food processor. Puree mixture to a fine paste, adding water a little at a time as needed for consistency. Set aside until needed.

Chicken:
Heat oil in a large skillet. Add chicken and shallot and stir-fry over low heat, turning chicken occasionally until lightly browned on all sides. Stir in curry paste. Add tomatoes and chicken stock and stir thoroughly. Bring to a simmer, reduce heat and continue simmering until chicken is done and sauce is thickened, about 20 minutes. Add jalapeño, season with *garam masala*, cayenne pepper, and salt. Continue simmering for 5 minutes. Serve on individual plates and top each serving with a pat of butter.

East India

East India straddles the border of India and Bangladesh, with the Indian portion designated as the states of West Bengal, Assam, Arunachal Pradesh, Nagaland, Meghalaya, Tripura, Manipur and Mizoram. The state of West Bengal extends from the Himalayas in the north to its coastline along the Bay of Bengal to the south. The landscape of West Bengal is defined largely by the forested Chota Nagpur Plateau and the Sundarbans Delta wetlands. Much of India's far eastern region is located in the Himalayas and is bordered by Nepal, Bhutan, and Bangladesh to the west, by Tibet and China to the north, and by Myanmar to the east.

The cuisine of this region has a long culinary history, with British, French, Chinese, Afghan, Muslim, Anglo-Christian, and Jewish cultural influences. East Indian flavors are characterized by the use of mustard oil and a traditional five-spice blend of cumin, onion seed (nigella), fennel seed, fenugreek, and mustard seeds. Seafood (especially fish) with rice and lentils are the primary staples. Fruits and vegetables include gourds, roots, leafy greens, eggplant, onions, beans, okra, pumpkins, plantains, banana blossoms, and jackfruit. The cuisine also includes unleavened bread and is known for its exquisite confections. In many settings, meals are served European-style in consecutive courses, rather than all at once, as in other regions of India.

For my East Indian recipe, I have chosen Bengali Catfish, a colorful curry seasoned with a blend of earthy Bengali spices and vibrant aromatics that bring the flavor of the plump, meaty catfish fillets to life. Served with a classic rice pilaf, it's an especially memorable main course for an Indian meal.

Curry Asia!

Bengali Catfish

Serves 4

Curry Paste:
4 cloves garlic, peeled and coarsely chopped
1 knob gingerroot, peeled and coarsely chopped (about 1 tablespoon)
1 shallot, peeled and coarsely chopped
1 jalapeño pepper, seeded and coarsely chopped
2 teaspoons cumin
2 teaspoons coriander
2 teaspoons turmeric
1/4 teaspoon cayenne pepper (more or less to taste)
1/4 cup water (as needed)

Fish:
2 pounds catfish or basa filets, cut into generous chunks
1 tablespoon peanut oil

Curry:
1 teaspoon nigella (onion seeds)
1 teaspoon yellow mustard seeds
1 teaspoon fennel seeds
1 small onion, peeled and thinly sliced
Curry paste (see recipe)
1 cup chicken stock
3 large tomatoes, cored and coarsely chopped (about 4 cups)
2 jalapeño peppers (red, green, or both), seeded and thinly sliced

Curry Paste:
Place all ingredients except water in a blender or food processor. Puree mixture to a fine paste, adding water a little at a time as needed for consistency. Set aside until needed.

Fish:
Heat oil in a wok or large skillet. Add fish and fry until golden brown on both sides. Remove from the heat and set aside.

Curry:
Heat oil in a wok or large skillet. Add nigella, mustard, and fennel seeds and fry until they begin to pop. Add onion and sauté until tender. Add curry paste and stir to thoroughly mix. Stir in chicken stock and tomatoes and bring to a simmer. Reduce heat and continue simmering for about 20 minutes, stirring occasionally, until slightly thickened. Add catfish pieces and jalapeño peppers to the sauce and simmer uncovered for about 5 minutes. Serve with rice pilaf or plain steamed rice.

Bangladesh

The independent nation now known as Bangladesh used to be part of India. What was once the Indian state of Bengal now straddles the border of India and Bangladesh, with the Indian portion designated as the state of West Bengal. In 1947, when Pakistan declared independence from British rule, East Bengal became East Pakistan. In 1971, East Pakistan declared its independence from Pakistan and was renamed Bangladesh. But despite the shifting geopolitical boundaries, much of the original Bengali culture and cuisine remain intact.

The geography of Bangladesh is largely defined by the vast network of rivers that courses through its landscape. The mighty Padma (Ganges), Jamuna (Brahmaputra) and Meghna Rivers, as well as hundreds of lesser tributaries, flow down from the Himalayan highlands to the Bay of Bengal, forming a fertile floodplain, a huge delta, and a marshy coastline.

Much of the country lies at sea level along the Tropic of Cancer, and is prone to dramatic weather patterns, including heavy monsoons, widespread flooding, devastating cyclones, and periodic droughts. Agriculture is a major industry for the cultivation of fruits, vegetables, and grains. Modest highlands are found inland where bamboo, sugarcane, and rubber trees flourish.

As in East India, the cuisine of Bangladesh has a long culinary history, with British, French, Chinese, Afghan, Muslim, Anglo-Christian, and Jewish cultural influences. It is also further divided into regional cuisines, each with its own style and flavors. In the southern region, along the coastline, seafood is major component. The central Dhaka region is known for its meat and rice dishes. Spicy vegetable curries are common to the west and northwestern regions. In the northeast, freshwater fish, pickled vegetables, and fruit are the most common indigenous ingredients. The most popular Bangladeshi seafood dish is called *panta illish*, a large platter of fried *hilsa* and dried *shutki* fish with *panta bhat* (fermented rice), and side dishes of *daal* (lentils), onions, and green chilies.

Beef is unique to Bangladeshi cuisine since the Hindu population in neighboring Bengal does not eat beef. The cuisine also includes unleavened bread and is known for its exquisite confections. Aromatics and spices most commonly used in Bangladeshi cuisine are garlic, ginger, coriander, cumin, turmeric, mustard seeds, and chilies. Desserts are typically spiced with cardamom and cinnamon.

Bangladeshi curries are characterized by the use of mustard oil and a traditional five-spice blend of cumin, nigella (onion seeds), fennel seeds, fenugreek, and mustard seeds. Seafood, especially fish, is a favorite main ingredient. *Illish* (hilsa), a salt-water species that migrates to fresh water for spawning, is the most popular food fish in Bangladesh. Carp, catfish, and shrimp or prawns are also popular choices for Bangladeshi curries.

For my Bangladeshi dish, I've chosen seafood *dopeaja*, a spicy seafood curry that will make your taste buds sit up and take notice. The spice paste is a classic Bangladeshi blend, in a tomato-based sauce with lots of whole shrimp, scallops, and chunks of fish.

Curry Asia!

Bangladeshi Seafood Dopeaja

Serves 4

Whole Spices:
1 teaspoon cumin seeds
1 teaspoon fennel seeds
1 teaspoon mustard seeds
1/2 teaspoon nigella (onion seeds)
1/2 teaspoon dried chili flakes

Curry Paste:
1 large knob gingerroot, peeled and coarsely chopped
1 large shallot, peeled and coarsely chopped
2 green jalapeño peppers, de-seeded and coarsely chopped
1 teaspoon paprika
1 teaspoon turmeric
Whole spice powder (see recipe)
1/4 cup water (more or less as needed)

Main Ingredients:
1 tablespoon ghee (substitute clarified butter)
Curry Paste (see recipe)
2 large tomatoes, cored and coarsely chopped
1/2 pound firm white fish (catfish, basa, tilapia, etc.), cut into large chunks
1/2 pound medium shrimp, peeled and deveined, tails intact
1/2 pound small scallops
2 jalapeño peppers, seeded and thinly sliced
4 scallions, thinly sliced
1 small bunch cilantro, coarsely chopped (about 1/3 cup)

Whole Spices:
Combine all spices in a spice grinder or mortar and grind to a fine powder. Set aside until needed.

Curry Paste:
Place all ingredients except water in a blender or food processor. Puree mixture to a fine paste, adding water a little at a time as needed for consistency. Set aside until needed.

Main Ingredients:
Heat ghee or butter in a large skillet. Add curry paste and sauté until the mixture is fragrant and almost dry. Stir in tomatoes and bring to a simmer. Reduce heat and continue simmering until sauce is slightly thickened. Add fish, shrimp, scallops and jalapeños and continue simmering until shrimp are pink and tender and fish is done. Stir in scallions and cilantro, simmer briefly and serve immediately with steamed rice and flatbread.

Indian Subcontinent Side Dishes

No Indian curry meal would be complete without one (if not several) of these enticing side dishes. Mulligatawny Soup is a fine way to start, and the Spicy Watermelon Rind and Green Chili Chutney is one of my favorite accompaniments for Indian curry.

Curry Asia!

Spicy Watermelon-Rind and Green Chili Chutney

1 medium watermelon with a thick rind
1 cup sugarcane vinegar
1 cup water
1 cup sugar
1 knob gingerroot, peeled and finely shredded (about 1 tablespoon)

4 cloves garlic, peeled and minced
2 jalapeño peppers, seeded and minced
1 teaspoon dried red chili flakes
1 teaspoon salt

Cut the watermelon in half lengthwise, and then into 1-inch slices. Remove the flesh of the watermelon, leaving a thin layer of the pink fruit on the rind. Thinly pare away the green skin and discard. Chop the watermelon rind into 1/2-inch cubes. The amount of rind will vary depending on the size of your watermelon, but for this recipe you will need about 10 cups of 1/2-inch cubes.

To make the chutney, combine watermelon rind with all other ingredients in a large pot and stir to mix. Bring the mixture to a boil, reduce heat, and simmer until the sugar syrup is thickened and the watermelon rinds are translucent. Stir frequently and check often to ensure that the liquid doesn't boil dry. This may take up to 2 hours. When the chutney is done, it should resemble a fruit jam with only a little liquid syrup remaining. The total quantity will be about 2 cups. Remove chutney from heat and set aside to cool. Ladle into sterilized glass jars with tight-fitting lids. Chutney will keep in the refrigerator for up to a month.

Curry Asia!

Sinhalese Pickled Vegetables

1 teaspoon mustard seeds
2 cups vinegar
1/4 cup sugar
1 knob gingerroot, peeled and finely shredded
6 cloves garlic, peeled and coarsely chopped
1/2 teaspoon turmeric

1/4 teaspoon cayenne pepper
1 teaspoon salt
24 pearl onions, trimmed and peeled
2 carrots, thinly sliced
1 cup green beans, cut into 1-inch pieces
1 jalapeño pepper (red or green), seeded and minced

Grind the mustard seed and 1 teaspoon of the vinegar to a paste with a pestle and set aside. Pour remaining vinegar into a pan. Add the mustard paste, sugar, ginger, garlic, turmeric, cayenne pepper, and salt. Stir thoroughly. Bring to a boil. Add onions, carrots, beans, and jalapeño. Reduce heat and simmer until vegetables are just tender, about 10 minutes. Remove from heat and set aside to cool. Transfer to a clean jar with a tight-fitting lid. Refrigerate overnight to marry flavors.

Cook's Note: Sinhalese pickles may also be whirred in the food processor to make a tasty relish.

Curry Asia!

Tomato Cucumber Mint Raita

Serves 4

12 cherry tomatoes, halved
1 large cucumber, peeled, seeded, and thinly sliced

1 small bunch fresh mint leaves, coarsely chopped (about 1/4 cup)
2 cups plain yogurt

Combine all ingredients in a mixing bowl. Stir gently to thoroughly mix. Chill for one hour.

Curry Asia!

Curried Red Lentil Daal

Serves 4

Curry Paste:
1 shallot, peeled and coarsely chopped
4 cloves garlic, peeled and coarsely chopped
1 small knob gingerroot, peeled and coarsely chopped
1 green jalapeño pepper, seeded and coarsely chopped
1 teaspoon cumin
1 teaspoon coriander
1 teaspoon garlic powder
1/2 teaspoon dried red pepper flakes
1/2 cup coconut milk
1 lime, juice only

Red Lentil Daal:
2 cups chicken broth
1 cup split red lentils (dried)
Curry paste (see recipe)
Salt to taste

Curry Paste:
Combine all ingredients in a blender or food processor and puree to a fine paste. Set aside until needed.

Red Lentil Daal:
Combine broth and lentils in a saucepan and bring to a simmer. Reduce heat, and continue simmering for about 10 minutes, until lentils are tender. Drain and set aside. Bring curry paste to a simmer in a separate saucepan. Reduce heat and continue simmering for 10 minutes, stirring frequently. Stir in lentils and season with salt. Continue simmering for another 5 minutes, until mixture is thickened. Set aside to cool. Serve with rice or flatbread.

Mulligatawny

Serves 4

1 pound boneless chicken breasts or thighs, cut into 1/2-inch cubes

1 tablespoon ghee (substitute clarified butter)

1 small onion, peeled and coarsely chopped

2 cloves garlic, peeled and minced

4 cups chicken stock

1 can unsweetened coconut milk (13.5 ounces)

1 tablespoon curry powder

Salt to taste

Heat the ghee in a soup kettle over medium heat. Sauté the chicken pieces until lightly browned. Remove chicken from the kettle, and set aside. In the same kettle, add onion and garlic and stir-fry until tender. Add the chicken stock and simmer uncovered for 20 minutes. Remove from heat and set aside to cool. Pour the broth into a food processer and puree until smooth. Strain the broth back into the kettle through a fine sieve. Add coconut milk, curry powder, and chicken. Simmer uncovered for another 20 minutes, stirring frequently.

The Origins of Mulligatawny Soup

It's funny…I've always thought the word mulligatawny sounded vaguely Irish, but I know well that it is a distinctively Indian soup that gets its name from the Tamil language. The two words that form the name as we know it in English are *millagu* and *thanni*, which together mean pepper water. But my mulligatawny research indicates that it is actually much closer to a Tamil soup called *rasam* than to the one they call *millagu thanni*.

Although the true origins of mulligatawny date much further back into Indian culinary history, its contemporary origins stem from a diluted version of a rustic pea and lentil stew, adapted during the colonial era to suit British requests for a soup course in their daily meals.

Over time, each outpost and household rendered its own version of mulligatawny, and a much wider variety of ingredients such as meats, vegetables, fruits, and coconut milk came into play. Mulligatawny made its way to England, where it remains as a delicious reminder of the British Raj.

I fell in love with my very first spoonful of mulligatawny while on a romantic dinner date at Gaylord's in San Francisco in 1986, and I've been making it in my own kitchen ever since. Nothing esoteric, mind you…just a basic recipe made with chicken stock and coconut milk, seasoned with a heaping tablespoon of curry powder.

Awhile back, I even made a batch using a recipe from *The Raffles Hotel Cookbook*. The process was so complex that it took me two days of chopping, sautéing, simmering, straining, reducing, and seasoning to finally render it ready to ladle into bowls. And once I did, to my amusement, I found that the rarefied Raffles recipe wasn't all that much better than my own humble version. But I must say that it was an interesting exercise in following a gourmet recipe to the letter.

Curry Asia!

Sri Lankan Spiced Rice

Serves 4

Sri Lankan Curry Powder:
1 teaspoon cumin seeds
1 teaspoon coriander seeds
1 teaspoon fennel seeds
1/2 teaspoon fenugreek seeds
1/2 cinnamon stick, coarsely crushed
6 green cardamom pods
6 cloves
3 curry leaves

Spiced Rice:
3 tablespoons peanut oil
2 cups basmati rice
1 onion, peeled and chopped
4 cloves garlic, peeled and minced
1 knob gingerroot, peeled and finely
    shredded (about 1 tablespoon)
1 teaspoon Sri Lankan Curry Powder (see
    recipe)
1 stick whole cinnamon
6 whole cardamom pods
3 whole cloves
1/4 cup golden raisins
3 cups water
1/4 cup cashews, coarsely chopped

Sri Lankan Curry Powder:
Combine all ingredients in a heavy skillet and place over low heat, gently shaking the pan until the spices are fragrant and lightly toasted. Remove from the heat and set aside to cool. Transfer toasted spices to an electric grinder, blender, or stone mortar and grind to a fine powder. Set aside until needed.

Spiced Rice:
Preheat oven to 400 degrees. Heat the oil in a large pan or baking dish with a tight-fitting lid. Add rice, onions and garlic and stir-fry until onion is tender and rice is opaque. Stir in ginger, curry powder, cinnamon, cardamom pods, cloves, and raisins. Add water and bring to a simmer. Cover and bake for about 30 minutes, until rice is tender and liquid is absorbed. Remove rice from the oven, fluff with a fork (removing whole spices if desired), and stir in cashews.

Puffed Flatbreads

Serves 4

1 cup flour	1/2 cup water
1/4 teaspoon salt	1 tablespoon vegetable oil

Combine flour, salt, and water in a mixing bowl and stir to form a ball of dough. More water may be added a little at a time as needed to form the dough. Place dough on a floured surface and knead vigorously for about 5 minutes, until the dough is smooth and elastic. Roll the dough into a ball and place in a bowl covered with a damp kitchen towel. Set aside to rest for 30 minutes.

Divide the dough into 4 equal portions and shape into balls. On a lightly floured surface, roll each ball of dough into a 6-inch round about 1/8 inch thick. Lightly brush the flatbreads with oil and place on a non-stick baking sheet. Keep flatbreads covered with a slightly damp kitchen towel until needed.

Preheat oven broiler. Place baking sheet with flatbreads on the top rack, about 6 inches from the broiler. Leave the oven door ajar and carefully monitor the flatbreads as they bake. When the flatbreads are puffed and lightly browned on the top, remove the pan from the broiler, turn the flatbreads over and return to the broiler to brown on the other side. When flatbreads are done, remove from the broiler and serve immediately.

Love Me…Love My Flatbread

Throughout many years of experimenting with international foods, I have attempted various types of flatbreads with roulette-like results. I never know whether it's going to do what it's supposed to do, from forming a pita pocket to puffing up like a balloon. On rare occasions, it comes out perfect: lightly crisp, with an airy cavity in the center. But more often, it's a disappointment, if not a downright disaster.

When it comes to my flatbreads, I'm reminded of a passage from *Illusions*, one of my favorite books by Richard Bach. In it, Donald Shimoda describes the panbread Richard makes over his campfire. "It's sort of like…a fire…after a flood…in a flour mill, don't you think?"

Love me…love my flatbread…

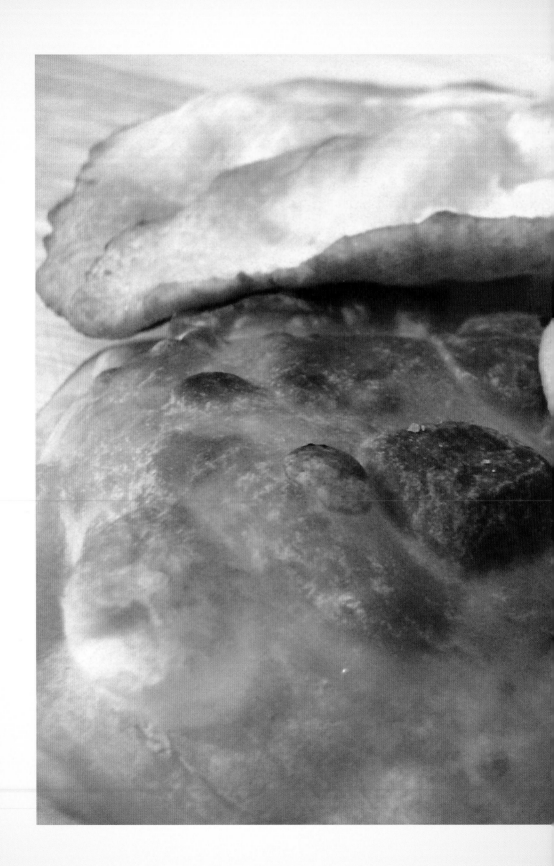

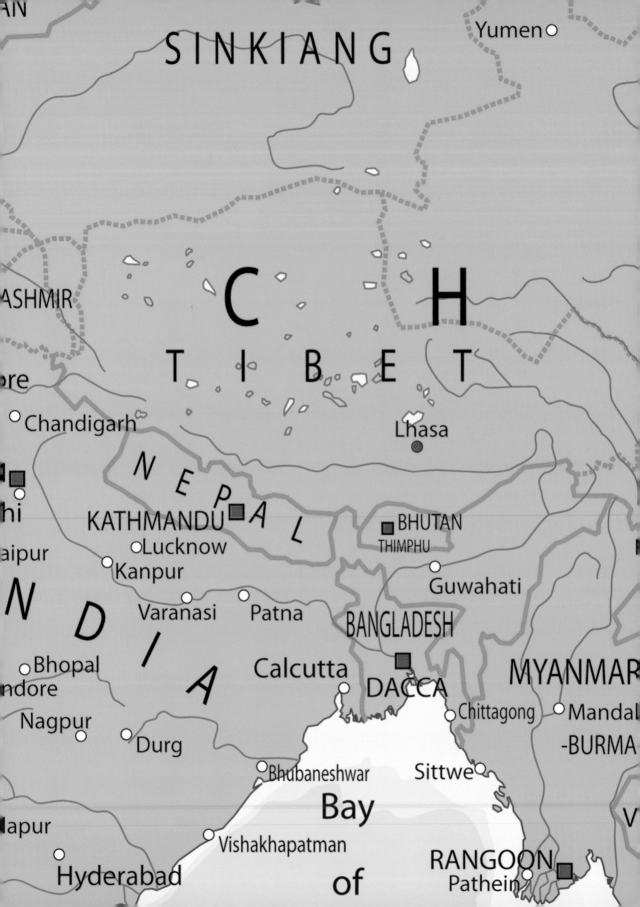

The Himalayas

Having made my way throughout the Indian subcontinent, I'm ready to scale the peaks of the Himalayas to taste the curries of Nepal, Tibet, and Bhutan. Unlike its subcontinental neighbors, the Himalayan landscape offers limited terrain for agriculture, which is markedly reflected in its rustic curries. Agricultural scarcity notwithstanding, Himalayan curries are rich and hearty, with strong affinities for both warming winter stews, and vibrant vegetarian curries to please the palates of Buddhist ascetics.

Nepal

Nepal is a small, land-locked nation located high in the Himalayas, surrounded by India, Tibet, and Bhutan. At only 57,000 square miles, much of its geography is defined by the world's highest mountain range, with Mount Everest within its borders. At lower elevations, the landscape descends sharply through the forested hill region to a fertile floodplain known as the Terai.

Although the ingredients used to prepare Nepali cuisine are quite common, Nepali food is unique in flavor. The basic ingredients include rice, wheat, corn, lentils, meat, and fresh indigenous vegetables. Spices and aromatics include garlic, onions, scallions, ginger, turmeric, cumin, coriander, nutmeg, bay leaves, black pepper, Szechuan peppercorns, chilies, cilantro, and mustard oil.

A typical Nepali curry meal might feature an appetizer, a hearty soup, a meat dish, one or more vegetable side dishes, *achar* (Nepali chutney), a rice dish, a flatbread, and a beverage such as beer, a strong spirit, or yogurt lassi, then finally, dessert with tea.

The curries of Nepal are hearty, spicy, and simple. The predominant flavor elements include the basics: garlic, ginger, onions and chilies, with cumin, coriander, turmeric, and *garam masala* to add spice. With some of the Buddhist population excluding meat from the daily diet, many curry dishes feature vegetables as the main ingredient. However, meat curries may feature lamb, mutton, goat, or chicken. Sauces and marinades may also include yogurt.

To represent the curries of Nepal, I've created a dish made with goat. A common Nepali main ingredient, goat is similar to lamb in both flavor and texture. My recipe features a yogurt marinade spiced with a traditional Nepali garam masala.

Nepali Goat Curry

Curry Paste:

4 cloves garlic, peeled and coarsely chopped
1 knob gingerroot, peeled and coarsely chopped (about 1 tablespoon)
1/2 onion, peeled and coarsely chopped
1 tomato, cored and coarsely chopped
1 jalapeño pepper, seeded and coarsely chopped
1 tablespoon cumin
1 tablespoon coriander
1 teaspoon turmeric
1 teaspoon red chili flakes (more or less to taste)
1/4 cup water (as needed)

Nepali Garam Masala:

1 teaspoon cumin seeds
1 teaspoon coriander seeds
3 cardamom pods
1/2 teaspoon black peppercorns
2 whole cloves
1/2 teaspoon ground cinnamon
1/4 teaspoon ground nutmeg

Nepali Goat Curry:

3 pounds goat meat (with or without bones), cut into chunks
2 cups yogurt
Nepali curry paste (see recipe)
2 tablespoons peanut oil
1/2 onion, peeled and thinly sliced
2 cups water
2 jalapeño peppers, seeded and thinly sliced
Nepali garam masala

Curry Paste:

Place all ingredients except water in a blender or food processor. Puree mixture to a fine paste, adding water a little at a time as needed for consistency. Set aside until needed.

Nepali Garam Masala:

Toast cumin, coriander, cardamom, peppercorns, and cloves in a heavy skillet over low heat until fragrant and lightly browned. Cool and transfer to a spice grinder. Add cinnamon and nutmeg and grind the mixture to a fine powder. Set aside until needed.

Nepali Goat Curry:

Combine 3 tablespoons of the curry paste with yogurt. Add goat pieces and stir to thoroughly coat. Cover and marinate in the refrigerator for 4 hours, or overnight. At cooking time, remove meat from the marinade and drain over the bowl to remove excess liquid. Save remaining marinade for the sauce.

Heat oil in a large kettle. Add goat and onion and stir-fry until meat is browned and onions are tender. Stir in marinade and remaining curry paste, add water and bring to a simmer. Reduce heat, cover and simmer about 1 hour. Stir in jalapeños and *garam masala* and continue simmering uncovered until sauce is thickened, about 20 minutes. Serve with steamed rice.

Cook's Note: Goat is typically available at Filipino, Middle Eastern, and Mexican markets with in-house butcher shops. If goat is unavailable in your area, this recipe works equally well with lamb as the main ingredient.

Tibet

The Tibetan landscape does not produce an abundance of agriculturally-farmed or naturally occurring edible flora and fauna. As a result, Tibetan food is significantly limited compared to that of neighboring countries such as India and China. Its range of flavors and methods of preparation are less varied than those of other Asian cuisines.

With the prevalence of Tibetan Buddhism as the country's main religion, vegetarian food is common, using ingredients such as grains, potatoes, and leafy greens. However, the Tibetan diet also includes meats and dairy products, especially those produced by yaks, which are native to the mountainous terrain. These ox-like creatures are raised for meat as well as for their milk, which makes a pungent cheese.

Spicy curries, similar to those of India, are commonly featured at the Tibetan table. However, Tibetan curry tends to be simple, often vegetarian, with a comparatively limited palette of spices that typically includes dried chilies, cumin, turmeric, and fenugreek, with garlic, onions, and ginger for the aromatics. Many Tibetan curries also include tomatoes and potatoes, two New World vegetables that have found their way into the Himalayan diet. Tibetan curry meals are usually accompanied by rice and simple flatbreads.

For my Tibetan curry dish, I have created a recipe for a hearty, simple dumpling soup with yak as the main ingredient. Although yak is quite common in Tibet, it is exotic to most Western diets. While not abundantly available in neighborhood markets, it can be purchased through online meat merchants.

Curry Asia!

Tibetan Yak Curry and Dumpling Soup

Serves 4

Curry Paste:
1/2 onion, peeled and coarsely chopped
4 cloves garlic, peeled and coarsely chopped
1 jalapeño pepper, seeded and coarsely
  chopped
1 large tomato, cored and coarsely chopped
1 teaspoon turmeric
1 teaspoon cumin
1 teaspoon chili garlic paste (more or less,
  to taste)

Broth:
2 tablespoons vegetable oil
2 pounds boneless yak, cut into bite-sized
  pieces (substitute beef or lamb)
1/2 onion, thinly sliced
Curry paste (see recipe)
1/4 cup soy sauce
8 cups water

Dumplings:
1-1/2 cup flour
3/4 cup water

Curry Paste:

Combine curry paste ingredients in a blender or food processor and puree to a fine paste. Set aside until needed.

Broth:

Heat the vegetable oil in a large wok over medium heat. Add meat and onions and stir-fry until meat is lightly browned and onions are translucent. Stir in curry paste and soy sauce. Add water and bring to a simmer. Cover and continue simmering for 40 minutes.

Dumplings:

While the broth is simmering, mix the flour and water into a smooth ball of dough. Set aside to rest for 20 minutes. On a lightly floured surface, roll dough into a large flat sheet about 1/8 inch thick, dusting with more flour as needed. Using a sharp knife or pizza cutter, cut the dough lengthwise into 1-inch strips, and crosswise into 1-inch squares.

When the broth has simmered for 40 minutes, add the dumplings a few at a time, stirring occasionally to separate. Simmer for another 20 to 30 minutes until dumplings are soft and tender. Ladle the soup into individual serving bowls. Serve with flatbread.

Bhutan

Bhutan means Land of the Thunder Dragon, but at only about 15,000 square miles, it is one of the world's smallest countries. Its dramatic geography is defined by the eastern Himalayas;,a landlocked nation, Bhutan is bordered by Tibet to the north, and India to the south.

Bhutan's climate is harsh, with much of its landscape remaining perpetually frozen, and the lower altitudes often beset with snowstorms and high winds. Bhutan's climatic cycle also includes hot summers and a rainy season that causes frequent landslides. Its alpine geography is deeply carved by snow-fed rivers and provides limited opportunity for agriculture, although there are regions of grassland and sub-tropical forests in the foothills, where rice is widely cultivated.

Much of Bhutan's population is Buddhist and many are vegetarian. Yak is the preferred meat among non-vegetarians, but chicken and pork are also common in Bhutanese cuisine. Rice is an important staple, along with wheat, which is made into *puta* noodles. Fresh produce includes garlic, onions, scallions, ginger, cilantro, pumpkins, white radish, potatoes, cabbage, cauliflower, lentils, and beans.

The most commonly used spices and flavoring agents are turmeric, cumin, coriander, nutmeg, asafoetida, fenugreek, bay leaves, Szechuan peppercorns, sesame seeds, soy sauce, vinegar, and mustard oil. Many of Bhutan's classic dishes are spiced with red chili peppers of the *capsicum annuum* variety.

The curry I've chosen to represent Bhutan is a popular dish called called *jasha maroo*. This recipe yields a hearty chicken stew that is both flavorful and filling.

Jasha Maroo

Serves 4

Curry Paste:
4 cloves garlic, peeled and coarsely chopped

1/2 small onion, peeled and coarsely chopped

1 jalapeño pepper, seeded and coarsely chopped

1 large tomato, cored and coarsely chopped

1 teaspoon cumin

1 teaspoon coriander

1 teaspoon turmeric

1 teaspoon crushed red chili flakes (more or less to taste)

Jasha Maroo:
2 tablespoons peanut oil

2 pounds boneless chicken thighs or breasts, cut into bite-sized pieces

3 cloves garlic, peeled and minced

1 medium onion, thinly sliced

1 small leek, white part only, thoroughly rinsed and finely chopped

1 ounce *shaoxing* (Chinese rice wine)

Curry Paste (see recipe)

1 large tomato, cored and coarsely chopped

1 teaspoon crushed red chili flakes (more or less to taste)

2 cups chicken stock

2 jalapeño peppers, seeded and thinly sliced

Curry Paste:
Combine all ingredients in a blender or food processor and puree to a fine paste. Set aside until cooking time.

Jasha Maroo:
Heat the oil in a large skillet or wok. Add chicken, garlic, onion, and leek and sauté until lightly browned. Add shaoxing and curry paste and stir thoroughly. Stir in tomato, dried red chili flakes, and chicken stock. Simmer uncovered over low heat for about 30 minutes, until chicken is tender and sauce is thickened. To finish, add jalapeños and continue simmering until peppers are just tender, about 5 to 7 minutes. Serve with wild rice and flatbread.

Himalayan Side Dishes

This collection of Himalayan side dish recipes offers a tempting array of flavors and textures, including the ubiquitous Ema Datshi (a spicy cheese dip), Momo Dumplings, a hearty Lamb and Barley Soup, Pickled Red Cabbage and Cauliflower Salad, Chow Chow Noodles, Green Bean and Potato Tema, and a Wild Rice Medley.

Curry Asia!

Ema Datshi

Serves 4

2 tablespoons vegetable oil
1 large onion, peeled and finely chopped 4
  cloves garlic, peeled and minced
4 jalapeño peppers, seeded and thinly
  sliced
1 pound feta cheese, crumbled

1 cup water (more or less as needed)
Salt to taste
Cilantro for garnish
1 package flatbread (pita, naan, etc.), cut
  into wedges and lightly toasted

Heat vegetable oil in a saucepan over medium heat. Add onion, garlic and jalapeños and stir-fry until tender and lightly browned. Reduce the heat, add feta cheese and stir until the cheese melts. Add water a little at a time, until the mixture reaches a creamy consistency. Season with salt. Transfer to a serving dish and garnish with cilantro. Ema Datshi may be served warm or at room temperature, with flatbread for dipping.

Momo Dumplings with Tomato Achar

Tomato Achar:

4 cloves garlic, peeled and coarsely chopped

1 knob gingerroot, peeled and coarsely chopped (about 1 tablespoon)

3 red jalapeño peppers, trimmed and coarsely chopped

2 tomatoes, cored and coarsely chopped

2 tablespoons toasted sesame seeds

1 teaspoon cumin

1 small bunch cilantro (about 1/2 cup)

Momo Dipping Sauce:

1/4 cup soy sauce

1/4 cup vinegar

1 teaspoon chili oil

Momo Dumplings

Filling:

1/2 pound ground lamb (substitute yak or beef)

4 scallions, thinly sliced

3 cloves garlic, peeled and minced

1 knob gingerroot, peeled and finely shredded (about 1 tablespoon)

2 red jalapeño peppers, trimmed and minced

1 ounce shaoxing (Chinese rice wine)

2 teaspoons flour

2 teaspoons soy sauce

1 teaspoon turmeric

1 teaspoon cumin

1 package round wonton wrappers

Several large lettuce or cabbage leaves for lining the steamer basket

Tomato Achar:

Combine all ingredients in a food processor and puree to a fine texture. Transfer to dipping dishes and serve with Momo Dumplings.

Momo Dipping Sauce:

Combine all ingredients in a jar with a tight fitting lid, shake vigorously and let stand for 1 hour to marry flavors.

Momo Dumplings

Filling:

Combine filling ingredients in a bowl and knead by hand until thoroughly and uniformly mixed. To assemble the dumplings, place a spoonful of the filling in the center of each wonton wrapper.

Dumplings may be formed in two styles. For a half-moon shape, fold the wrapper in half over the filling and pinch the edges to seal. For a sachet style dumpling, pinch the dough into a series of tiny pleats, gathering the edges together into a tightly puckered rosette at the top.

Line a bamboo steamer or the bottom of a large skillet with lettuce or cabbage leaves. Top with dumplings and steam over boiling water for 30 minutes. If using a skillet, add just enough water to cover the bottom of the pan beneath the leaves. Check the water level frequently throughout the cooking process and replenish water as needed. Remove the dumplings from the steamer and serve immediately with Achar and Dipping Sauce. Makes about 3 dozen dumplings.

Alternate Cooking Method: Heat 2 tablespoons of vegetable oil in a large skillet or wok. Fry the dumplings in the hot oil until the bottoms are brown and crispy. Add 1/4 cup water, cover pan and steam over low heat for about 7 minutes, until filling mixture is done and dumplings are tender.

Cook's Note: Depending on the size of your pan, you may have to fry/steam the dumplings in two batches. In this case, you will need extra oil and/or water for each batch.

Lamb and Barley Soup

Serves 4

2 tablespoons vegetable oil
1 pound boneless lamb, cut into small pieces
4 cloves garlic, peeled and minced
1 knob gingerroot, peeled and finely shredded (about 1 tablespoon)
1 onion, peeled and finely chopped
2 jalapeño peppers, seeded and thinly sliced
8 cups lamb or beef stock (see recipe in the Resources chapter)

1 cup barley
1 teaspoon cumin
1 teaspoon coriander
1 teaspoon turmeric
1 teaspoon crushed red chili flakes (more or less to taste)
2 cups mushrooms, thickly sliced
1 large tomato, cored and coarsely chopped
2 cups spinach, coarsely chopped

Heat oil in a large soup kettle. Add lamb, garlic, ginger, onion, and jalapeño and sauté until lamb is browned and onions are tender. Add stock, barley, cumin, coriander, turmeric, and chili flakes and bring to a boil. Reduce heat and simmer for about 45 minutes, until barley is just tender. Add mushrooms, tomatoes, and spinach and continue simmering for about 15 minutes.

Cook's Note: If this soup is not served immediately, the barley will continue to absorb the soup broth and may need more stock added at serving time.

Curry Asia!

Pickled Red Cabbage and Cauliflower

1 small head red cabbage, cored and cut into 1/2- inch strips
4 jalapeño peppers, seeded and thinly sliced
1/4 cup kosher salt

1 cup rice wine vinegar
1 tablespoon sugar
1 tablespoon chili oil (more or less to taste)
2 cups cauliflower florets

Place the cabbage in a large colander over a large empty bowl to catch juices. Sprinkle with 3 tablespoons of kosher salt and set aside for 2 hours. Place the jalapeño strips in a separate colander or sieve over an empty bowl to catch juices, sprinkle with 1 tablespoon of kosher salt and set aside for 1 hour. Thoroughly rinse the cabbage and jalapeños and transfer to two separate containers with tight-fitting lids to prevent the red cabbage from discoloring the peppers.

In a measuring cup, combine vinegar, sugar, and chili oil. Stir until sugar is dissolved. Pour 3/4 cup of the mixture over cabbage, and 1/4 cup over the jalapeños, cover both containers and refrigerate overnight. Shake or turn the containers every few hours to ensure even marinating. At serving time, combine the cabbage and jalapeños, transfer to a serving dish and arrange with cauliflower florets.

Cook's Note: For a softer texture, cauliflower florets may be lightly blanched or steamed and chilled before serving. And if you wish, they may also be cured in a separate container with the same salt and vinegar pickling process as the cabbage and peppers.

Curry Asia!

Chow Chow Noodles

Serves 4

2 tablespoons vegetable oil

1 pound boneless chicken, cut into bite-sized pieces

4 cloves garlic, peeled and minced

1 knob gingerroot, peeled and finely shredded (about 1 tablespoon)

1 onion, peeled and coarsely chopped

4 red jalapeño peppers, trimmed and finely chopped

1/4 cup soy sauce

1 teaspoon turmeric

1 tomato, cored and coarsely chopped

1 carrot, peeled and thinly sliced

1 cup green beans, cut into 1" lengths

2 cups spinach leaves

4 portions long noodles, cooked according to package directions

2 cups chicken broth

Heat oil in a large wok over medium heat. Add chicken, garlic, ginger, onion, and peppers, and stir-fry until chicken is browned and onions are tender. Stir in soy sauce and turmeric. Add tomato, carrot, and green beans and simmer until tender, about 5 minutes. Add spinach and toss gently until wilted. Add noodles and chicken broth and bring to a simmer. Remove from heat, cover and set aside for about 10 minutes before serving.

Cook's Note: After cooking and draining, noodles may be tossed with a little oil to prevent them from sticking. For spicy noodles, I like to use chili oil.

Curry Asia!

Green Beans and Potato Tema

Serves 4

2 tablespoons peanut oil

4 medium-sized red potatoes, thickly julienned (like French fries)

1 small onion, thinly sliced

2 cloves garlic, peeled and minced

1 knob gingerroot, peeled and finely shredded (about 1 tablespoon)

2 jalapeño peppers, seeded and thinly sliced

2 cups green beans, cut into 2" lengths

1 large tomato, cored and coarsely chopped

1 teaspoon chili garlic sauce (more or less to taste)

2 tablespoons soy sauce

Heat the oil in a wok or large skillet over medium heat. Add the potatoes and onions and stir-fry until they begin to brown. Add garlic, ginger, jalapeños, and green beans and continue stir-frying until the beans and potatoes are just tender. Add tomatoes, chili sauce, and soy sauce, bring to a simmer, and continue stir-frying until beans and potatoes are done. If the mixture becomes to dry, a little water may be added.

Curry Asia!

Wild Rice Medley

Serves 4

2 cups uncooked wild and brown rice mix, prepared according to package directions

2 tablespoons butter

1 small leek, white part only, rinsed and finely chopped, about 1/4 cup

1/2 onion, finely chopped

2 cloves garlic, peeled and minced

1 cup chicken stock

Salt and pepper to taste

Prepare the rice according to package directions in a rice cooker or large saucepan with a tight-fitting lid. Melt the butter in a large skillet or wok. Add leek, onion and garlic and sauté until tender. Add cooked rice and stir to blend. Add chicken stock, reduce heat to low and simmer, stirring frequently, until stock is absorbed, about 5 to 10 minutes.

Southeast Asia

Southeast Asia occupies a large peninsula that includes Myanmar, Thailand, Cambodia, Laos, Vietnam, and part of Malaysia. Geographically, nearly all of Southeast Asia falls well within the Tropic of Cancer, and is therefore tropical in climate and abundant in agriculture. This, combined with its rich cultural melting pot, makes for a vibrant array of curry possibilities.

NƯỚC MẮM NHĨ

Việt Hương

HIỆU BA CON CUA

VIET HUONG FISHSAUCE COMPANY, INC.

上羊
三蟹嘜
調味佳品
惜香豐富

生產商及總發行
越香有限公司

魚汁·蝦·水·果糖及水解蛋白質

THREE CRABS Brand ®

頭遍魚露

PREMIUM FIRST EXTRACT FISH SAUCE

프리미엄 숄멸치예젓

GREDIENTS: ANCHOVY EXTRACT (FISH), SALT, WATER,
FRUCTOSE & HYDROLYSED WHEAT PROTEIN

H PHẦN: NƯỚC MẮM NHĨ, MUỐI, NƯỚC, ĐƯỜNG & PROTEIN L

Net 10.14 FL.Oz.[0Pt.6FL.Oz.]300ml

淨容量:10.14安士(0品脫6安士)300毫升

YAN WAI YUN CO., LTD.

THAI

Fish

SAUCE

HEALTHY BOY BRAND

肥兒標鮮魚露

NET CONTENTS 250 ML. (8 fl.oz.)

THAI
heritage
Fish sauce
特級魚露

泰水

200 ml
245 g

Spotlight on Spice: Asian Fish Sauce

Asian fish sauce goes by many names. In Vietnam, it's called *nuoc mam*. In Thailand, it's known as *nam pla*; in Cambodia, *toeuk trey*; in Indonesia, *ketjap ikan*; in the Philippines, *patis*; in Korea, *aek jeot*, and in Japan, *shottsuru*.

Soy sauce evolved from Chinese fish sauce. Fish sauce has been documented in the history of ancient Rome, where it was known as *garum*. Even English Worcestershire sauce evolved from fish sauce.

Asian fish sauce is made from fermented fish. Depending on the source or the ethnic culture, it may be freshwater or saltwater, fresh or dried, from a single species, or from an amalgam of various fish. One of the most common types is made from anchovies. Some fish sauces contain only fish and salt, while others are flavored with herbs and spices.

The production process involves rinsing, draining, salting, and layering fish into wooden barrels (or in the case of mass production, into industrial-sized vats), and fermenting for up to a year. The mixture is then filtered, aired in the sunlight, and bottled. The end product is an intensely fishy, salty, amber-colored liquid with a high protein content. Depending upon the number of multiple fermentations each batch of fish undergoes, there are varying grades of quality, with the first, single fermentation being the best.

Fish sauce may be used in many dishes from nearly every Asian cuisine, including condiments, soups, sauces, and stir-fry recipes. An Asian market will likely carry several different brands of fish sauce, and you may be uncertain which one to buy. However, fish sauce is usually so economically priced, you can buy one of each and try them all.

Myanmar

Formerly known as Burma, the nation of Myanmar is located on the Southeast Asian peninsula. It is bounded on the northeast by China, on the east by Thailand, to the northwest by East India and a small shared border with Bangladesh, and by the Andaman Sea and the Bay of Bengal along its southwestern coast. Yangon (Rangoon) and Mandalay are its major cities.

Comparable in size to the state of Texas, the geography of Myanmar has two distinct regions. The upper region is defined by forested highlands that reach altitudes of 5,000 feet, while the lower is characterized by coastal plains traversed by the Ayeyarwaddy (formerly Irrawaddy) River network. Indigenous vegetation includes pine, oak, and rhododendron in the highlands, and in the lowlands bamboo, teak, rubber, mangrove, coconut, betel palm, citrus, mango, guava, and banana.

With the three rich cultures of China, India, and Thailand surrounding Myanmar, its cuisine has many culinary influences. Its lengthy coastline provides seafood as an abundant culinary ingredient. Burmese cuisine also includes beef, chicken, and pork, as well as a variety of fruits and vegetables that grow on fertile floodplains and in tropical forests. Rice is a key component of the daily diet, along with noodles and tofu. Flavoring agents include tamarind, lime, ginger, coconut milk, *la phet* (fermented tea leaves), *ngapi* (shrimp paste), salty bean paste, fish sauce, and vinegar.

A typical meal includes rice as the primary ingredient, with side dishes of meat or seafood curry, a vegetable stew, pickled fish, noodle salad, *palata* flatbread, various condiments, and a light soup that serves as a beverage, with fresh fruit or traditional confections for dessert. Religion also plays an important role in the cuisine of Myanmar, with Muslims avoiding pork and some Buddhists preferring a vegetarian diet.

Due to its proximity to India, Myanmar's cuisine includes a rich variety of curries, although they are somewhat milder and less complex than their Indian counterparts. Many feature coconut milk as the liquid component, while some include oil in large quantities. Chicken, shrimp, fish, and pork are common main ingredients, while flavoring agents include garlic, ginger, onion, fish sauce, tamarind, green chilies, mango, turmeric, and cayenne pepper. One of Myanmar's most popular curries is a noodle dish called *Ohn-no khaut swè*, curried chicken and wheat noodles in coconut milk.

Curry Asia!

Mandalay Pork and Green Mango Curry

Serves 4

Curry Paste:

4 cloves garlic, peeled and coarsely chopped

1 knob gingerroot, peeled and coarsely chopped (about 1 tablespoon)

1/2 small onion, peeled and coarsely chopped

1 unripe mango, peeled, cored, and coarsely chopped

2 kaffir lime leaves (optional)

1 jalapeño pepper, seeded and coarsely chopped

1 tablespoon fish sauce

1/4 cup water (more or less as needed)

Pork Curry:

2 tablespoons peanut oil

Curry paste (see recipe)

2 pounds boneless pork ribs, cut into bite-sized pieces

2 cups pork stock (substitute chicken stock)

1 teaspoon dried red chili flakes (more or less to taste)

1 can unsweetened coconut milk (13.5 ounces)

2 limes, juice only

Curry Paste:

Place all ingredients except water in a blender or food processor. Puree mixture to a fine paste, adding water a little at a time as needed for consistency. Set aside until needed.

Pork Curry:

Combine curry paste and pork in a bowl. Stir to thoroughly mix, cover and refrigerate for 2 hours, or overnight. Transfer pork to a colander and drain away excess marinade over the bowl. Reserve excess marinade for the sauce. Heat oil in a large skillet or wok. Add pork and stir-fry until pan is almost dry and pork is lightly browned. Stir in remaining marinade, add pork stock and chili flakes and bring to a simmer. Reduce heat and continue simmering uncovered for about 30 minutes, stirring occasionally. Stir in coconut milk and lime juice and continue simmering for about 20 minutes, until pork is tender and sauce is thickened. Serve with steamed rice.

Rangoon Chicken Noodle Curry

Serves 4

Curry Paste:
4 cloves garlic, peeled and coarsely chopped
1 knob gingerroot, peeled and coarsely chopped (about 1 tablespoon)
1/2 small onion, peeled and coarsely chopped
1 jalapeño pepper, seeded and coarsely chopped
1 tablespoon fish sauce
1 teaspoon turmeric
1/4 cup water (as needed)

Chicken Broth:
4 chicken thighs, skin and bones intact
1 tablespoon peanut oil
Salt to taste

Soup:
1/2 cup *besan* (chickpea flour)
1 cup water
6 cups chicken broth
1 can unsweetened coconut milk (13.5 ounces)

Noodles:
4 portions long noodles (vermicelli, linguine, ramen, etc.)
1 tablespoon peanut oil

Garnishes:
4 hard-boiled eggs, peeled and sliced
1 medium onion, soaked in water and finely sliced
1 small bunch cilantro, coarsely chopped
1 cup crispy chow mein noodles
2 limes, cut into wedges
Dried red chili flakes
Fish sauce

Curry Paste:
Place all ingredients except water in a blender or food processor. Puree mixture to a fine paste, adding water a little at a time as needed for consistency. Set aside until needed.

Chicken Broth:
Heat oil in a large kettle. Add chicken, skin side down, and fry until lightly browned. Fill the kettle with water, season with salt and bring to a boil. Reduce heat and simmer for about 45 minutes, until chicken is done and tender. Remove chicken pieces and strain broth through a fine sieve to remove sediment. When chicken is cool, discard skin and bones, coarsely chop chicken and set aside.

Soup:

Combine besan with water and whisk until smooth. In a large kettle, combine chicken broth, besan mixture, and coconut milk and bring to a simmer. Reduce heat and continue simmering, stirring occasionally until soup is slightly thickened, about 30 minutes. Add chopped chicken, remove from heat and set aside.

Noodles:

While the soup is simmering, prepare noodles according to package directions. Drain, toss with oil, cover and set aside until serving time.

Garnishes:

Arrange all garnishes on serving dishes and place on the table for guests to help themselves.

To Assemble:

Place one portion of noodles in each soup bowl. Ladle soup and chicken over the noodles. Serve with garnishes.

Spotlight on Spice: Kaffir Lime

The kaffir lime tree is native to the Indian subcontinent, nearly all of Southeast Asia, and Indonesia. Its botanical designation is *Citrus hystrix*. It is valued for both its rough-skinned citrus fruit and its fragrant leaves, which have an unusual figure-eight shape. This thorny bush grows to a height of two to three feet and is well-suited to container cultivation.

The leaves and fruit of the kaffir lime are widely used in Asian cuisine. Kaffir lime leaves are pleasantly fragrant and flavorful; they are used to impart a uniquely citrus-like component in many Southeast Asian and Indonesian dishes. The limes themselves are quite small. The juice is intensely acidic, so it is preferred for its medicinal qualities rather than for use in cooking. The rind, however, is pleasantly fragrant. Both the fruit and the leaves are also available dried or frozen. When added fresh to broth or sauces, the rind is typically grated into zest, and the leaves are usually chopped into fine slivers. Dried leaves may be added whole, or they may be rehydrated in warm water. Dried kaffir lime peel may be added to broth and sauces in large pieces.

Thailand

Thailand is located in Southeast Asia on the same peninsula as Burma, Cambodia, Laos, and Vietnam. Its main landmass is a spacious inland region that descends southward into a narrow peninsula, which it shares with Myanmar and Malaysia. It is bordered by the Gulf of Thailand to the east and the Andaman Sea to the west. At an elevation of only a few feet above sea level, the heart of the country is flat and fertile, with abundant irrigation from the Mekong, Nan, Yom, Ping, and Wang Rivers.

The north is mountainous, with peaks rising to 8,500 feet (2,590 meters), ranging south along the Myanmar border to the west. The northern region is heavily forested with teak trees. The east and northeast are defined by the Korat plateau and the Phetchabun Mountains. There the climate is dry, and livestock is the primary product. The narrow southern peninsula, which includes the island of Phuket, is mountainous and covered with tropical jungles.

Agriculture is the primary industry of Thailand, with rice as its most abundant crop. Among Thailand's other agricultural products are corn, tapioca, and sugarcane. Fishing, both marine and freshwater, is one of Thailand's most essential industries as the Thai people rely on seafood for much of their sustenance.

Thailand's proximity to India and China has had a strong influence on its cuisine, however, Thai cuisine has its own distinctive characteristics. Although the majority of Thai people are Buddhist, a significant number are Muslim and Hindu with their own distinctive culinary specialties. Many commercially packaged foods are prepared and labeled to conform to Islamic dietary laws, foodstalls throughout Thailand conform to halal standards, and Indian restaurants are plentiful.

Thai cuisine includes many of the same ingredients used in other Southeast Asian dishes: lots of hot chili peppers, a similar assortment of spices, and many of the same herbs and fresh ingredients. Rice is the primary starch, and is usually topped with modest amounts of curry and other spicy sauces. Noodles are also served in abundance. Since Thailand is a coastal nation, seafood is commonly featured in many Thai dishes. Two flavoring ingredients, an Asian fish sauce called *nam pla* and a shrimp paste called *kapi* are essential elements of nearly every dish.

Thai cuisine is also flavored with ginger, garlic, onions, tamarind, hot chili peppers, cilantro, basil, lemongrass, peanuts, kaffir lime leaves, cumin, black pepper, palm sugar, coconut milk, and sesame oil. A typical Thai dish combines the four basic flavor elements: sweet (sugar, fruits, sweet peppers), spicy hot (chilies), sour (vinegar, lime juice, tamarind), and salty (soy sauce, fish sauce, shrimp paste).

Nearly every Thai cookbook begins with basic recipes for three curry pastes: red, green, and yellow. These pungent concoctions are featured in the ingredient lists for all kinds of recipes. Regardless of the color, the basic ingredients of Thai curry pastes include garlic, ginger, shallots, lemongrass, coriander, cumin, and shrimp paste. Red curry paste includes lots of red chilies. Green curry paste gets its vibrant color from green chilies and cilantro. Yellow curry paste turns a brilliant shade of ochre with the addition of turmeric or curry powder. All are rich and spicy, and may be used in a variety of dishes.

To represent Thai curry, I have chosen dishes made with each of the three basic curry pastes: a vibrant Green Curry Chicken, a golden Yellow Curry Shrimp, and a fiery Red Curry Beef; plus a rich and hearty Muslim-style Massaman Beef Curry.

Spotlight on Spice: Thai Chiles

Several of the dishes in this recipe collection call for Thai chilies, and in making them, I had to prepare the chilies for cooking. This meant handling them while trimming, removing seeds and membranes, chopping, and adding them to the bowl or cooking pan. Although I've handled jalapeños and poblanos in the past, this was my first experience with the Thai variety and I had no idea what to expect.

Only green Thai chilies were available at my favorite produce market, no red. My experience with jalapeños is that once they turn red, they are considerably more peppery than they are in their green phase. Even though the Thai chilies were green, I had no idea what I was in for. Given my delicate palate, I figured one chili for each recipe would be enough. So I put three green Thai chilies on the cutting board and proceeded to trim, clean and chop them.

I had been warned in the past to wear gloves when handling chilies, but did I listen? No. I'm hard-headed about things like that and, never having had any worse misadventure from handling jalapeños than a forgetful swipe of my eyelid afterwards, I chose to ignore those warnings. So…note to self: Be sure to wash hands thoroughly and don't touch your eyes after handling the chilies.

Onward I went with the Thai chilies. Trim trim trim...Scrape scrape scrape... Chop chop chop...Wash hands with lots of soap. No problem. Then back I went to my sofa to watch a movie while my dishes marinated with the chilies.

Despite my cursory precautions, about a half hour later, I suddenly found myself drenched in sweat and up to my elbows on fire with the peppery burn of the chilies. WHAT THE...?

Before I started to panic, I went on the Internet and found a Scoville chart with the ascending ratings of all the various types of chilies. GADZOOKS!!! Thai chilies have a Scoville rating of 100,000 to 300,000, compared to the wimpy jalapeños I'm used to, at only 2,500 to 5,000.

Okay...NOW it was time to panic. For the next couple of hours, I tried to keep a lid on it, wondering how much worse it would get, whether or not I would break out in hives or blisters, and whether I should call the hospital for reassurance. Fortunately, reason prevailed, and the sting of the peppers gradually subsided.

Amazingly, when it comes to Thai chilies, it's truly the seeds and membranes that pack all the punch. Once those are removed, Thai chilies are the pussycats of peppers. But I've definitely learned my lesson. Next time, I'll wear gloves. And one of these days when I'm feeling brave, I might actually try eating a Thai chili in its bad-ass entirety: seeds, membranes and all.

Thai Green Curry Chicken

Serves 4

Green Curry Paste:
2 stalks lemongrass, lower half only, trimmed and coarsely chopped
2 green jalapeño peppers, seeded and coarsely chopped
1 small bunch cilantro (about 1 cup)
1 knob gingerroot, peeled and coarsely chopped (about 1 tablespoon)
4 cloves garlic, peeled and coarsely chopped
1 large shallot, peeled and coarsely chopped
1 teaspoon cumin
1 teaspoon coriander
1 tablespoon nam pla (fish sauce)
2 limes, juice only
1/4 cup water (as needed)

Thai Green Curry Chicken:
1 tablespoon peanut oil
2 pounds boneless, skinless chicken breasts or thighs, cut into 1" pieces
1 small onion, peeled and thinly sliced
Green Curry Paste (see recipe)
2 cups chicken stock
1 can unsweetened coconut milk (13.5 ounces)
2 jalapeño peppers, seeded and thinly sliced
2 limes, cut into wedges
Fresh cilantro

Green Curry Paste:
Place all ingredients except water in a blender or food processor. Puree mixture to a fine paste, adding water a little at a time as needed for consistency. Set aside until needed.

Thai Green Curry Chicken:
Heat oil in a large kettle or wok. Add chicken and onion and stir-fry until lightly browned. Add curry paste and stir thoroughly to mix. Stir in chicken stock and bring to a simmer. Reduce heat and simmer for 30 minutes, stirring occasionally, until chicken is tender and sauce is thickened. Add coconut milk and jalapeños and continue simmering for about 10 minutes, until peppers are just tender. Serve with steamed rice, and garnish with fresh cilantro and lime wedges.

Curry Asia!

Thai Yellow Curry Shrimp

Serves 4

Yellow Curry Paste:

2 stalks lemongrass, lower half only, coarsely chopped
6 cloves garlic, peeled and coarsely chopped
1 knob gingerroot, peeled and coarsely chopped (about 1 tablespoon)
1 small shallot, peeled and coarsely chopped
1 jalapeño pepper, seeded and coarsely chopped
2 kaffir lime leaves (optional)
1 teaspoon coriander
1 teaspoon cumin
1 teaspoon turmeric
1 tablespoon mild curry powder
1 tablespoon fish sauce
1 lime, juice only
1/4 cup water (as needed)

Thai Yellow Curry Shrimp:

1 tablespoon peanut oil
1 large shallot, peeled and thinly sliced
Yellow curry paste (see recipe)
1 can unsweetened coconut milk (13.5 ounces)
4 dozen medium shrimp, peeled and deveined, tails intact
2 jalapeño peppers, seeded and thinly sliced
1/2 cup flaked coconut, lightly toasted

Yellow Curry Paste:

Place all ingredients except water in a blender or food processor. Puree mixture to a fine paste, adding water a little at a time as needed for consistency. Set aside until needed.

Thai Yellow Curry Shrimp:

Heat oil in a wok. Add shallots and stir-fry until tender and translucent. Add curry paste and continue stir-frying for about 1 minute. Stir in coconut milk and bring to a simmer. Reduce heat, cover and simmer for 30 minutes. Add shrimp and jalapeños and continue simmering until shrimp are pink and jalapeños are tender, about 5 to 7 minutes. Serve over steamed rice and sprinkle with toasted coconut.

Curry Asia!

Thai Red Curry Beef

Serves 4

Red Curry Paste:

3 red Thai chilies, coarsely chopped
1/2 red bell pepper, trimmed, seeded and coarsely chopped
1 stalk lemongrass, lower half only, trimmed and coarsely chopped
1 knob gingerroot, peeled and coarsely chopped (about 1 tablespoon)
4 cloves garlic, peeled and coarsely chopped
1 shallot, peeled and coarsely chopped
1 teaspoon cumin
1 teaspoon coriander
1 tablespoon nam pla (fish sauce)
1 lime, juice only
1 tablespoon peanut oil
1/4 cup water (as needed)

Thai Red Curry Beef:

2 pounds boneless beef, cut into 1" pieces
1 tablespoon peanut oil
1/2 onion, peeled and thinly sliced
Red Curry Paste (see recipe)
2 cups beef stock
1/2 red bell pepper, trimmed, seeded, and thinly sliced
1 teaspoon dried red chili flakes (more or less to taste)

Red Curry Paste:

Place all ingredients except water in a blender or food processor. Puree mixture to a fine paste, adding water a little at a time as needed for consistency. Set aside until needed.

Thai Red Curry Beef:

Combine beef with 1/4 cup of red curry paste, cover and marinate for 2 hours or overnight. Heat oil in a large kettle or wok. Add beef and stir-fry until pan is almost dry and meat begins to brown. Add onions and continue stir-frying until onions are translucent and meat is browned. Add remaining curry paste and stir thoroughly to mix. Stir in beef stock and bring to a simmer. Reduce heat and continue simmering for 40 minutes, stirring occasionally. Remove cover, add bell peppers and red chili flakes, Continue simmering for 20 minutes, until beef is tender and sauce is thickened. Serve with steamed rice.

Massaman Beef Curry

Serves 4

Whole Spices:
1 tablespoon coriander seeds
1 teaspoon cumin seeds
3 whole cloves
6 cardamom pods

Curry Paste:
4 cloves garlic, peeled and trimmed
1 knob gingerroot, peeled and coarsely chopped (about 1 tablespoon)
1 small shallot, peeled and coarsely chopped
1 stalk lemongrass, lower half only, coarsely chopped
Whole spice powder (see recipe)
1/2 teaspoon cinnamon
1/2 teaspoon nutmeg, freshly grated
3 Thai chilies, coarsely chopped (more or less to taste)
1 lime, juice only
2 tablespoon nam pla (fish sauce)
1/4 cup tamarind water
1 tablespoon palm sugar (substitute brown sugar)

Massaman Beef Curry:
1 tablespoon peanut oil
2 pounds boneless beef, cut into 1" pieces
1 small onion, peeled and thinly sliced
Massaman curry paste (see recipe)
1 can unsweetened coconut milk (13.5 ounces)
2 cups beef stock
2 medium potatoes, peeled and cut into 1" pieces
1/4 cup unsalted peanuts
1/2 cup spinach leaves, cut into chiffonade for garnish

Whole Spices:

Toast whole spices in a small skillet until lightly browned and fragrant. Set aside to cool. Transfer to a spice grinder and grind to a fine powder. Set aside until needed.

Curry Paste:

Combine all ingredients in a blender or food processor and puree to a fine paste. Set aside until needed.

Massaman Beef Curry:

Heat oil in a large kettle or wok, add beef and stir-fry until meat begins to brown. Add onions and continue stir-frying until onions are translucent and lamb is browned. Add curry paste and stir to thoroughly mix. Add coconut milk and beef stock and bring to a simmer. Cover and simmer for 30 minutes. Uncover, add potatoes and peanuts and continue simmering for 30 minutes, until potatoes are tender and sauce is thickened. Serve in individual bowls and garnish with spinach chiffonade.

Laos

Laos is a landlocked nation, sandwiched between Thailand and Vietnam. The Mekong River forms the border with Thailand, and the mountainous Annamite Chain geographically separates it from Vietnam. Only a small percentage of the Laotian landscape is suitable for agriculture, much of which is ideally suited for the cultivation of rice and the production of livestock.

Other agricultural products include bamboo, leafy herbs, and garden vegetables, as well as indigenous fruits such as mango, papaya, guava, pineapple, banana, coconut, orange, apple, grape, melon, tamarind, and the more exotic durian, mangosteen, jackfruit, soursop and langsat.

Among the more common and familiar Lao herbs and spices are ginger, galangal, chili peppers, garlic, shallot, lemongrass, basil, mint, and coriander. Fresh vegetables and fruits include Lao eggplant, green papaya, bamboo shoots, cloud ear mushrooms, long beans, tomato, cucumber, tamarind, and lime.

The flavors of Lao food are based upon the same sweet, sour, bitter, salty components found in other Southeast Asian cuisines. However, Lao food is unique in its interpretation, and texture is a key element. Many Lao dishes incorporate large amounts of fresh leafy herbs and vegetables, some of which are unfamiliar to western markets, gardens, and kitchens. Among them are wild betel leaves, yanang leaves, kaffir lime leaves, scarlet wisteria, banana blossoms, ginger blossoms, water spinach, acacia, tamarind leaves, curry leaves, and two bitter herbs: Piper ribesioides, and a bitter green called phak lin may, for which there appears to be no English translation. Other ingredients common to Lao food, but exotic to western markets are padaek fish paste, dried water buffalo skin, and a nori-like seaweed paper called kaipen.

Grilling, boiling, stewing, and steaming are the most common cooking methods. Cooking utensils to prepare a Lao meal are simple: a mortar and pestle, a charcoal brazier, a wok, a soup kettle, and a bamboo steaming basket. Favorite Lao dishes include laap (larb), a spicy mixed salad of meat, herbs and greens; tam mak hoong, a spicy green papaya salad; and Lao pho, a savory noodle soup. Sticky rice is served at nearly every meal, as is the ubiquitous Lao chili paste. Favorite desserts include steamed rice in banana leaf, coconut custard cake, and sweet steamed pumpkin. Beverages include Lao coffee with condensed milk, green tea, beer, and a fermented rice alchoholic beverage called lao lao.

Curry takes on a whole new meaning at the Lao dinner table, where fresh herbs and greens abound, sticky rice in round woven baskets is used as a vehicle to transport bites of food with the fingers, and a fiery chili paste called jaew bong stands at the ready to rev up the palate.

Lao curry can be as basic as fish and vegetables in broth, as elaborate as a Thai-inspired coconut milk elixir called kaeng kalee, or as simple as grilled fish or meat served with vibrant curry dipping sauces.

Meals are served on low rattan tables called ka toke. Spoons are used to eat soups, and chopsticks are used to eat noodles, but most Lao dishes are eaten with the hands or scooped with leafy greens, and are therefore served at room temperature. A typical meal includes soup, a grilled dish, a stew, a variety of fresh raw greens, an array of spicy dips and condiments, and sticky rice, all of which are served at the same time.

The dishes I've chosen to represent Lao curry are Broiled Tilapia with Green Curry Sauce, and Lao Curry Beef. The Broiled Tilapia is a perfect example of the Lao custom of serving the main course with copious quantities of leafy green herbs and a variety of flavorful condiments. And the recipe for the Lao Curry Beef is actually intended for cooking water buffalo. But beef is used here, since it is similar in taste and texture, and much more readily available. Ginger and jalapeños give the dish its peppery spice; the fish sauce provides a salty, savory component; and a splash of lime just before serving brightens the broth with a hint of citrus.

Curry Asia!

Broiled Tilapia with Green Curry Sauce

Serves 4

Green Curry Sauce:

1 tablespoon peanut oil

1 stalk lemongrass, bottom half only, coarsely chopped

2 kaffir lime leaves (optional)

1 jalapeño pepper, seeded and coarsely chopped

4 cloves garlic, peeled and coarsely chopped

1 shallot, peeled and coarsely chopped

1 knob gingerroot, peeled and coarsely chopped (about 1 tablespoon)

1 can unsweetened coconut milk (13.5 ounces)

1 small bunch cilantro, leaves and stems (about 1 cup)

1 tablespoon nam pla (fish sauce)

2 limes, juice only (about 1/3 cup)

1 tablespoon sugar

Broiled Tilapia

1 tablespoon peanut oil

1 whole tilapia (substitute *basa*, *swai* (Vietnamese catfish), or trout), about 3 pounds, cleaned and scaled

1 small onion, peeled and thinly sliced

1 lime, thinly sliced

1 small bunch fresh herbs (mint, cilantro, dill, parsley, etc.)

Green Curry Sauce:

Heat oil in a saucepan. Add lemongrass, jalapeño, garlic, shallot and ginger and stir-fry until fragrant and tender, about 3 minutes. Add coconut milk and bring to a simmer. Reduce heat, cover and continue simmering for 20 minutes. Remove from the heat and set aside to cool. Transfer coconut milk mixture to a blender or food processor. Add cilantro, fish sauce, lime juice, and sugar and puree to a fine consistency. Set aside until serving time.

Cook's Note: For a spicy, more vibrant sauce, leave the seeds of the chili peppers intact, omit the coconut milk and puree the remaining ingredients in a blender or food processor without cooking. Add a little water if needed for consistency.

Broiled Tilapia

Preheat oven to 350 degrees. Rub the fish with oil and fill the cavity with layers of onion, lime slices, and herbs. Place on a foil-lined baking sheet and bake for 20 to 30 minutes (depending upon size and thickness of fish). For crisp skin, switch oven from bake to broil and brown the top side of the fish for about 5 minutes. Serve with green curry sauce and steamed rice.

Lao Curry Beef

Serves 4

Curry Paste:

1 shallot, peeled and coarsely chopped

1 knob gingerroot, peeled and coarsely chopped (about 1 tablespoon)

4 cloves garlic, peeled and coarsely chopped

1 jalapeño pepper, seeded and coarsely chopped

2 kaffir lime leaves (optional)

1 tablespoon nam pla (fish sauce)

1 lime, juice only

1 tablespoon curry powder

1 teaspoon dried red chili flakes (more or less to taste)

1/4 cup water (as needed)

Lao Beef Curry:

1 tablespoon peanut oil

2 pounds boneless beef, cut into bite-sized pieces

Curry paste (see recipe)

2 cups beef broth

1 tablespoon nam pla (fish sauce)

1 cup green beans, cut into 1-inch lengths

2 scallions, trimmed and thinly sliced

1 cup coconut milk

1 lime, juice only

1 bunch fresh herbs (mint, cilantro, watercress etc., trimmed and coarsely chopped)

Curry Paste:

Place all ingredients except water in a blender or food processor. Puree mixture to a fine paste, adding water a little at a time as needed for consistency. Set aside until needed.

Lao Beef Curry:

Heat oil in a large wok or a deep skillet. Add beef and stir-fry until lightly browned. Add curry paste and continue stir-frying until curry paste is fragrant and almost dry. Add beef stock and bring to a simmer. Reduce heat, cover and simmer for about 40 minutes, until beef is tender. Add green beans, scallions, and coconut milk and continue simmering uncovered for about 10 minutes, until beans are tender. Stir in lime juice and serve with sticky rice and fresh herbs.

Cambodia

Cambodia lies fully in the tropics, at the tip of the Southeast Asian peninsula, nestled in the crescent formed by the borders of Thailand, Laos, and Vietnam. Its western coastline lies along the Gulf of Thailand. The central landscape is defined by a huge inland lake called Tonle Sap, and is traversed north to south by the mighty Mekong River. The coastal lowlands are encircled by a network of mountain ranges that separate Cambodia from the rest of Southeast Asia.

Cambodia's tropical climate is ideal for the cultivation of rice, but when it comes to Cambodian food…anything goes. The bounty of ingredients in typical Cambodian dishes includes nearly every kind of vegetable, meat, and seafood imaginable. Condiments and spices are consistent with other Southeast Asian cuisines, including fish sauce, soy sauce, rice vinegar, coconut, lime, mint, coriander, basil, lemongrass, chili peppers, kaffir lime leaves, curry powder, and sesame oil. Many dishes are served with *tirk salouk*, tangy dipping sauces made with lime juice and fish sauce, seasoned with ginger, garlic, and chili peppers.

Ironically, however, Cambodian curry recipes are not nearly as abundant as those of their Southeast Asian neighbors. They typically contain shallots, garlic, chilies, lemongrass, galangal, and *krachai*, also known as finger root. Spices include cumin, turmeric, and fenugreek. Tamarind paste, shrimp paste, or fish paste are also used as additional flavoring agents.

The curry itself might contain chicken, pork, or seafood, along with a variety of fresh vegetables such as onions, green beans, sweet peppers, and potatoes. The sauce typically contains coconut milk, fish sauce, fresh lime juice, and sugar. Once the dish is finished, it may be served with either steamed rice or rice noodles, and lots of leafy greens and herbs.

For my Cambodian curry dish, I've created a recipe based on a caramelized sauce. This method involves browning sugar in oil and adding coconut juice instead of coconut milk. For the curry paste, I combined garlic, ginger, shallots, fresh green chilies, and lemongrass, to which I added cumin, turmeric, kaffir lime leaves, fish sauce, tamarind paste, and dried chilies.

I've also added a recipe for irresistibly delicious Cambodian Lettuce Wraps with Mahogany Pork Ribs. I started with plump boneless pork ribs, which I marinated and braised in soy sauce, brown sugar, and garlic, with a dash of my secret ingredient: cinnamon. Once the ribs were tender, I drained off the braising liquid, thickened it with a little cornstarch, and then used it as the basting sauce for the browning phase of the cooking process. The finished ribs are moist and tender, and browned to a deep mahogany in a richly-flavored glaze with just a whisper of cinnamon.

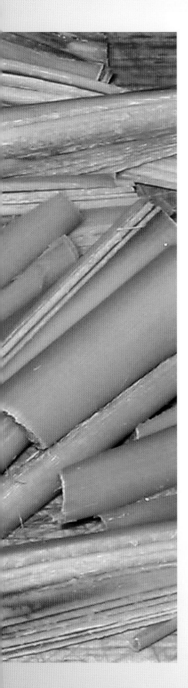

Spotlight on Spice: Lemongrass

Lemongrass is one of the most widely used elements in Asian, Caribbean, and African cuisines. Its scientific classification is *Plantae Magnokiophyta Liliopsida Poales Poaceae Cymbopogon*. There are more than fifty different species of lemongrass, which are also known as barbed wire grass, fever grass, citronella grass, silky heads, and *Hierba Luisa*. Lemongrass is a perennial, native to temperate and tropical climates, where it grows in thick tufts.

Lemongrass adds a citrus-like flavor to recipes, and may be fresh, dried, or powdered. Only the soft, inner core is edible, but the harder stalk may be crushed to release its flavor and aroma. Lemongrass is used to flavor teas, soups, and stews, and is also valued for its antiseptic and medicinal properties. As citronella grass, it is used as a mosquito repellent, as well as in perfumes, soaps, and candles.

Cambodian Caramelized Chicken Curry

Curry Paste:

3 tablespoons peanut oil
1 large shallot, peeled and coarsely chopped
4 cloves garlic, peeled and coarsely chopped
1 stalk lemongrass (lower half only), peeled and coarsely chopped
1 teaspoon cumin
1 teaspoon dried red chili flakes (more or less to taste)
1 knob gingerroot, peeled and coarsely chopped (about 1 tablespoon)
3 kaffir lime leaves (optional)

Caramelized Sauce:

2 tablespoons peanut oil
1/4 cup sugar
1 can coconut juice, warmed (do not use coconut milk)

Caramelized Chicken Curry:

2 pounds boneless, skinless chicken, cut into 1" strips
1 tablespoon fish sauce
2 tablespoons peanut oil
1 small onion, peeled and thinly sliced
Cambodian Curry Paste (see recipe)
Caramelized Sauce (see recipe)
1 cup tamarind water
2 jalapeño peppers, red or green, seeded and thinly sliced

4 portions rice noodles, or steamed rice, prepared according to package directions
2 limes, cut into wedges

Curry Paste:

Heat the oil in a wok and stir-fry all ingredients until fragrant and lightly browned. Set aside to cool. Transfer to a blender or food processor and puree to a smooth paste. Set aside until needed.

Caramelized Sauce:

Heat oil in a wok or skillet, with a tight-fitting lid standing ready. Add sugar and stir constantly until it dissolves and begins to brown. When sugar is golden brown, quickly and carefully add warmed coconut juice and cover immediately to protect from splattering oil. Remove from the heat, stir, and set aside until needed.

Caramelized Chicken Curry:

Combine chicken pieces with fish sauce and 1 tablespoon of the peanut oil. Stir to thoroughly coat and set aside to marinate for 1 hour. While the chicken is marinating, make the curry paste and caramelized sauce (see recipes).

To prepare the curry, heat the remaining tablespoon of peanut oil in a wok or large skillet. Add chicken and onions and stir-fry until chicken is lightly browned and onions are tender and translucent. Add curry paste and stir to uniformly mix. Stir in caramelized sauce and tamarind water and bring to a simmer. Cover and continue simmering for 40 minutes, until chicken is done and tender. Uncover and add jalapeños. Continue simmering for about 10 minutes, until peppers are tender. Serve immediately with fresh lime wedges and rice noodles or steamed rice.

Cook's Note: To make tamarind water, dissolve a teaspoon of tamarind paste in a cup of hot water. You may also substitute tamarind-flavored soda, which is available at Mexican markets or upscale grocery stores.

Curry Asia!

Cambodian Lettuce Wraps
with Mahogany Pork Ribs

Serves 4

Curry Paste:

2 cloves garlic, peeled and finely minced

1 knob gingerroot, peeled and coarsely chopped (about 1 tablespoon)

2 tablespoons soy sauce

2 tablespoons brown sugar

1 tablespoon sesame oil

1/2 teaspoon cinnamon

1/4 cup water (as needed)

Curry Pork Ribs:

2 pounds boneless pork ribs, cut into chunks

Curry Paste (see recipe)

1 tablespoon cornstarch dissolved in 1/4 cup water

1 head red leaf lettuce, washed and trimmed into individual leaves

Curry Paste:

Place all ingredients except water in a blender or food processor. Puree mixture to a fine paste, adding water a little at a time as needed for consistency. Set aside until needed.

Curry Pork Ribs:

Combine pork and curry paste in a large bowl and stir thoroughly. Cover and refrigerate for 4 hours, or overnight. Wrap pork and marinade in aluminum foil. Preheat oven to 275. Roast foil-wrapped pork for 2 hours. When pork is done, drain the drippings and marinade into a small saucepan. Bring to a boil, add cornstarch mixture and stir until thickened. Preheat oven broiler. Transfer pork to a foil-lined baking sheet. Brush pork with thickened sauce and broil until browned and lightly charred. Repeat brushing and turning to evenly brown and char on all sides. Remove from the oven and set aside to cool. Serve with lettuce leaves.

Vietnam

The geography of Vietnam is often likened to the long, S-shaped yoke of an ox, with a basket hanging from each end. To the north lies the Red River Delta, and to the south, the Mekong Delta, joined by a narrow, mountainous backbone in between. As a result, Vietnamese cuisine is distinctly regional, from the cooler northern region, the rich cultural Hue region in the center, and the tropical southern region, each with its own indigenous vegetables, seafood, and wildlife; each with its own style and spice.

Northern cuisine is lighter and less pungent; the cuisine of the central Hue region, once the site of the ancient capital, is flavorful and elaborate; while the southern region falls under the influence of Chinese cuisine, using more pungent spices and stir-fry techniques. The southern region is also the melting pot of French and Indian influences, characterized by curries, and European ingredients such as bread, potatoes, asparagus, shallots, and fine herbs.

The curries of Vietnam are most common in the southern region, where the cuisine has certain elements that reflect Indian influences. Vietnamese curries are also characterized by many of the same ingredients found in other Southeast Asian curries, especially Thai and Cambodian.

A Vietnamese curry paste typically begins with garlic, lemongrass, onions or shallots, and ginger or galangal. Spices may include cumin, coriander, turmeric, and dried chilies, along with other flavoring agents such as *nuoc mam (fish sauce)*, shrimp paste, and kaffir lime.

Seafood such as shrimp, crab, and fish are popular main ingredients, and sauces usually contain either coconut milk, or a sweetly caramelized elixir made with palm sugar and coconut juice.

According to tradition, I have chosen to infuse the alluring tropical flavors of my Vietnamese curry in the belly of a rustic clay pot. I've chosen shrimp as the main ingredient, and my sauce recipe has a coconut milk base with a curry paste of garlic, shallots, lemongrass, shrimp paste, palm sugar, kaffir lime, nuoc mam, turmeric, cumin, and dried chilies.

Curry Asia!

Vietnam Clay Pot Shrimp Curry

Serves 4

Curry Paste:
1 stalk lemongrass, bottom half only, peeled and coarsely chopped
4 cloves garlic, peeled and coarsely chopped
1 shallot, peeled and coarsely chopped
1 green jalapeño pepper, seeded and coarsely chopped
1 teaspoon dried red chilies (more or less to taste)
1 tablespoon mild curry powder
1 tablespoon *nuoc mam* (fish sauce)
1 tablespoon shrimp paste (optional)
1 tablespoon palm sugar (substitute dark brown sugar)
1/4 cup water (as needed)

Shrimp Curry:
1 tablespoon peanut oil
1 small onion, peeled and thinly sliced
Curry paste (see recipe)
1 can unsweetened coconut milk (13.5 ounces)
1 pound medium shrimp, peeled and deveined
2 jalapeño peppers (red and/or green), seeded and thinly sliced
2 limes, cut into wedges
6 cups steamed rice

Curry Paste:
Place all ingredients except water in a blender or food processor. Puree mixture to a fine paste, adding water a little at a time as needed for consistency. Set aside until needed.

Shrimp Curry:
Heat oil in a skillet or saucepan. Add onions and stir-fry until translucent and lightly browned. Add curry paste and continue stir-frying for about 1 minute. Stir in coconut milk and bring to a simmer. Fill the clay pot about halfway with the coconut milk mixture, leaving enough room to add shrimp later. Allow the coconut milk to warm the clay pot for about 3 minutes before placing on the stove burner. Bring the coconut sauce to a simmer over low heat, cover and continue simmering for about 15 minutes. Carefully uncover clay pot and stir in shrimp and jalapeños. Cover and simmer for about 5 to 7 minutes longer, until shrimp are pink and peppers are tender. Remove from heat and allow pot to cool slightly before uncovering. Serve over steamed rice, and garnish with fresh lime wedges.

Southeast Asian Side Dishes

Every time I serve Southeast Asian cuisine, I always make a variation of light and lovely Vietnamese rice paper rolls. Also included in this side-dish collection is a Hmong-inspired Baby Bok Choy Stir-Fry. Either or both would make an excellent accompaniment for the Clay-Pot Shrimp.

Rice Paper Summer Rolls with Grilled Basa and Mango

Serves 4

Spicy Lime Dipping Sauce:

1/4 cup rice vinegar
1/4 cup fish sauce
1/4 cup lime juice
1/4 cup water
1 tablespoon sugar
3 cloves garlic, peeled and minced
1 small knob of gingerroot, peeled and finely shredded (about 1 tablespoon)
1 small red chili pepper, trimmed, seeded and minced
1/4 cup crushed peanuts

Rice Paper Summer Rolls:

1/2 pound basa filets, grilled and coarsely chopped
2 ripe mangos, peeled and thinly sliced lengthwise
1 small bunch fresh mint leaves, finely chopped (about 1/2 cup)
1 package spring greens (about 3 cups)
12 rice paper wrappers

Spicy Lime Dipping Sauce:

Combine all ingredients in a jar with a tight-fitting lid. Shake vigorously and set aside for one hour, or overnight. Serve in shallow dishes for dipping Rice Paper Summer Rolls.

Rice Paper Summer Rolls:

Divide each of the filling ingredients into 12 equal portions. Fill a large, shallow dish with warm water and soak a rice paper wrapper until softened. Carefully transfer the wrapper to a dinner plate. Place one portion of each filling ingredient in compact layers on the lower half of the wrapper, leaving the edges empty for tucking and rolling. Fold the lower edge of the wrapper up and gently snuggle it around the filling. Fold in the left and right sides of the wrapper toward the center and roll cigar-style toward the upper edge. Cut roll in half on a diagonal angle, and place on an attractive serving dish. Repeat with the remaining wrappers and filling. Serve with Spicy Lime Dipping Sauce.

Curry Asia!

Baby Bok Choy and Red Pepper Stir-Fry

Serves 4

1 tablespoon rice wine
1/4 cup oyster sauce
1 teaspoon *sriracha* (more or less to taste)
1 pound thick-sliced bacon, cut into 1"
   pieces

1 small knob gingerroot, peeled and finely
   shredded (about 1 tablespoon)
4 cloves garlic, peeled and minced
8 baby bok choy
1 red bell pepper, cored and thinly sliced

Combine rice wine, oyster sauce, and sriracha in a small bowl, stir thoroughly, and set aside. Heat a wok or large skillet over medium heat and fry the bacon pieces until they brown and begin to crisp. Add ginger and garlic and stir-fry until tender and fragrant. Add bell pepper and bok choy and continue stir-frying until tender. Add sauce mixture and stir gently to evenly distribute. Remove from heat and serve immediately.

The Islands

Just off the coast of Southeast Asia, straddling the waters of both the Pacific and Indian Oceans, is a network of islands that includes Indonesia, Papua New Guinea, Brunei, and the Philippines. In this group, I have also included the mainland regions of Malaysia and Singapore, since they are geographically adjacent to and culturally influenced by Indonesia.

Malaysia

Malaysia is a geographically divided nation that includes a slender peninsula that extends from the southern tip of Thailand, and a sizeable region on the north coast of Borneo, as well as a constellation of smaller islands. Both the peninsular region and the island region feature vast tropical rainforests and mountain ranges of significant altitude. Malaysia lies in the southernmost latitudes of the Tropic of Cancer, just a scant five degrees north of the equator. Its equatorial climate is hot and humid year-round, with two distinct monsoon seasons.

Because of its proximity to both continental Asia and the Indonesian archipelago, Malaysian cuisine is highly influenced by many cultures, including Malay, Chinese, Indian, Indonesian and European. Spice pastes called *rempah* are the foundation of many Malaysian dishes, and the main flavoring agents include the aromatic trinity of garlic, ginger or galangal, and onions or shallots. Lemongrass, gingerroot, and chilies are also common components.

The kaleidoscope of spices includes cumin, coriander, turmeric, cardamom, cinnamon, cloves, nutmeg, and peppercorns. Fresh leaves such as pandan, *salam*, basil, and kaffir lime add their heady fragrances. Condiments such as soy sauce, vinegar, tamarind, and shrimp paste give depth and dimension to the gestalt.

The most popular main ingredients are seafood and chicken, and many Malaysian curries use coconut milk as the base for the sauce or soup. Another element that is unique to Malaysian curry is the use of candlenuts, pounded to a fine paste to add texture and flavor. However, candlenuts are not always available in markets outside Asia, and may be substituted with nuts of similar flavor such as macadamia, cashew, or peanuts. It is also important to note that candlenuts must not be eaten raw.

To represent the curries of Malaysia, I have created recipes for two of its most popular dishes: Seafood Laksa (a curried noodle soup), and Kapitan Curry Chicken, a flavorful dish created especially for the officials who represented Malaysian constituents under Dutch and Portuguese colonial rule.

Laksa Curried Noodle Soup

Serves 4

Laksa Spice Paste:

2 stalks lemongrass, lower half only, peeled and coarsely chopped

1 green jalapeño pepper, seeded and coarsely chopped

1 knob gingerroot, peeled and coarsely chopped

2 shallots, peeled and coarsely chopped

4 cloves garlic, peeled and coarsely chopped

1 small bunch cilantro, leaves and stems

1 teaspoon shrimp paste (optional)

1 tablespoon nam pla (fish sauce)

1 tablespoon peanut oil

1 lime, juice only

1 tablespoon curry powder

1 teaspoon dried chili flakes (more or less to taste)

1/4 cup water (as needed)

Seafood Curry:

1 tablespoon peanut oil

Laksa Spice Paste (see recipe)

4 cups chicken stock

1/2 pound medium shrimp, peeled and deveined, tails intact

1/2 pound small scallops

1/2 pound firm white fish, cut into 1" chunks

1 can unsweetened coconut milk (13.5 ounces)

4 servings long vermicelli noodles (wheat or rice), prepared according to package direction

Garnishes:

Bean sprouts

Chili garlic sauce

Cucumber julienne

Fresh herbs (mint, cilantro, Thai basil)

Egg omelet, finely shredded

Chili peppers, seeded and thinly sliced

Spring onions, finely sliced

Lime wedges

Laksa Spice Paste:

Place all ingredients except water in a blender or food processor. Puree mixture to a fine paste, adding water a little at a time as needed for consistency. Set aside until needed.

Seafood Curry:

Heat peanut oil in a large wok or skillet. Add spice paste and stir-fry until fragrant, about 1 minute. Pour in the chicken stock and bring to a boil. Reduce heat and simmer for 20 minutes. Stir in seafood and coconut milk and continue simmering for 10 minutes, until shrimp is pink, scallops are tender, and fish is done.

Garnishes:

To serve, divide the noodles into 4 large soup bowls. Spoon the chicken over the noodles and ladle in enough laksa sauce to fill the bowl. Serve with assorted garnishes.

Curry Asia!

Kapitan Curry Chicken

Serves 4

Curry Paste:
1 stalk lemongrass, lower half only, peeled and coarsely chopped
2 shallots, peeled and coarsely chopped
4 cloves garlic, peeled and coarsely chopped
1 knob gingerroot, peeled and coarsely chopped
1 teaspoon cumin
1 teaspoon coriander
1 teaspoon turmeric
1/2 teaspoon nutmeg
1/2 teaspoon cinnamon
1 teaspoon dried red chili flakes (more or less to taste)
1/4 cup nuts (macadamia, cashew, or peanuts)
1 teaspoon shrimp paste (optional)
1 teaspoon tamarind paste (optional)
1/4 cup water (as needed)

Kapitan Curry:
1 tablespoon vegetable oil
2 pounds skinless chicken thighs or breasts, cut into bite-sized pieces
1 small onion, thinly sliced
Kapitan curry paste (see recipe)
3 cups chicken stock
1 can unsweetened coconut milk (13.5 ounces)
2 jalapeño peppers, seeded and thinly sliced
1 lime, juice only

Curry Paste:
Place all ingredients except water in a blender or food processor. Puree mixture to a fine paste, adding water a little at a time as needed for consistency. Set aside until needed.

Cook's Note: Since shrimp paste imparts a strongly fermented flavor with a lingering aftertaste, it is listed as an optional ingredient, as is the tamarind paste, another strongly flavored ingredient.

Kapitan Curry:
Heat oil in a wok or large skillet. Add chicken and onions and stir-fry until lightly browned. Stir in curry paste to evenly coat chicken. Add chicken stock and coconut milk and bring to a simmer. Continue simmering over low heat, stirring occasionally, for 30 minutes, until sauce is thickened. Add jalapeños and continue simmering for about 10 minutes, until peppers are tender. Stir in lime juice and serve over steamed rice.

Singapore

Clustered at the southernmost tip of Southeast Asia, the sixty-three-island nation of Singapore revolves around an ultramodern, pristine-clean, metropolitan hub, which is connected to the Malay Peninsula by the 1,056- meter Johor-Singapore Causeway across the Straits of Johor. Much like its Malaysian and Indonesian neighbors, Singapore has been both historically and culturally touched by Malay, Chinese, Indian, Indonesian and European influences. All have left their thumbprints on the culinary ethos, which runs the gamut from the simple street fare dished up by thousands of sidewalk vendors to the *haute cuisine* on the menus of the fourteen dining establishments in the legendary Raffles Hotel.

Street food is an integral part of everyday life in Singapore, and the choices are seemingly endless. From steaming soups and spicy noodles, to savory kebabs and sticky rice treats steamed in banana leaves, hard-working and resourceful street vendors offer up their irresistible fare from carts and kiosks at all hours of the day and night. And for many residents of these vibrant cultures, the abundant and economically affordable array of street food is the sole source of sustenance.

Since Singapore shares so many culinary similarities with Malaysia and Indonesia, to represent Singaporean curry, I have chosen two of its most popular street foods: Chili Crab, Singaporean Curry Puffs, and Hokkien Curry Noodles.

Chili Crab dates back to the 1950s, when Madam Cher Yam Tian, one of Singapore's most famous street vendors, began selling these fiendishly spicy delights from her stall on the beach. Singaporean Curry Puffs are modeled after the meat-and-potato-filled empanadas that were first introduced to Asia by the Portuguese during colonial times. Hokkien Curry Noodles are Fujian-style noodles in a fiery stir-fry with shrimp and fresh vegetables.

Curry Asia!

Chili Crab

Serves 4

Curry Paste:
6 cloves garlic, peeled and coarsely chopped
1 large knob gingerroot, peeled and coarsely chopped (about 2 tablespoons)
2 shallots, peeled and coarsely chopped
2 tablespoons sugar
2 limes, juice only
1/2 cup ketchup
2 teaspoons *sambal oelek* (more or less to taste)
2 tablespoons soy sauce
2 tablespoons rice vinegar
1/4 cup water (as needed)

Chili Crab:
2 tablespoons peanut oil
2 large Dungeness crabs, parboiled, separated, and cracked
Curry paste (see recipe)
1 cup stock (fish, chicken, or vegetable)
4 scallions, thinly sliced
2 limes, cut into wedges

Curry Paste:
Place all ingredients except water in a blender or food processor. Puree mixture to a fine paste, adding water a little at a time as needed for consistency. Set aside until needed.

Chili Crab:
Heat the oil in a large wok or frying pan, add crab and stir-fry for about 3 minutes. Add curry paste and toss gently to coat the crab pieces. Add stock, reduce heat, cover and simmer for 5 minutes. Add scallions and continue simmering for 2 minutes. Remove from heat, transfer crab pieces to attractive serving dishes, ladle sauce over the crab and serve immediately with fresh lime wedges.

Cook's Note: For this recipe, I used Dungeness crabs from our local waters. Other varieties such as stone, king, snow, or blue crabs may also be used, with quantities adjusted for adequate portion size.

Singaporean Curry Puffs

Curry Paste:
1 shallot, peeled and coarsely chopped
1 knob gingerroot, peeled and coarsely chopped (about 1 tablespoon)
4 cloves garlic, peeled and coarsely chopped
1 jalapeño pepper, seeded and coarsely chopped
1 lime, juice only
1 tablespoon curry powder
1 teaspoon dried red chili flakes (more or less to taste)
1/4 cup coconut milk

Curry Filling:
1 tablespoon peanut oil
1 large boneless, skinless chicken breast, coarsely chopped
2 medium potatoes, peeled and diced
Curry paste (see recipe)
Salt to taste
1/3 cup frozen green peas

Curry Puffs:
1 package pie crust mix
Curry filling (see recipe)
Vegetable oil for frying

Curry Paste:
Combine all ingredients in a blender or food processor and puree to a fine paste. Set aside until needed.

Curry Filling:
Heat oil in a skillet. Add chicken and potatoes and stir-fry until lightly browned. Add curry paste and salt and continue stir-frying until chicken is done, potatoes are soft, and pan liquid is completely evaporated. Stir in peas, remove from heat, and set aside until needed.

Curry Puffs:
Prepare pie crust according to package directions. Divide dough into 12 equal portions, and roll into 4-inch rounds. Place about 2 tablespoons of filling in the center of each. Fold the pastry in half over the filling and crimp the edges to seal. Heat about 1 inch of oil in a wok or skillet. Add curry puffs a few at a time and fry, turning once, until golden brown on both sides. Remove curry puffs from oil and drain on paper towels. Makes one dozen.

Curry Asia!

Hokkien Curry Noodles

Serves 4

Curry Paste:
4 cloves garlic, peeled and coarsely chopped
1 knob gingerroot, peeled and coarsely chopped (about 1 tablespoon)
1 shallot, peeled and coarsely chopped
1 teaspoon chili garlic sauce (more or less to taste)
 cup water (more or less as needed)

Sauce:
2 cups chicken stock
1/4 cup soy sauce
2 tablespoons oyster sauce
2 tablespoons cornstarch dissolved in 1/4 cup water

Stir Fry:
1 tablespoon sesame oil
1 pound large shrimp, peeled and deveined
2 carrots, thinly sliced
2 jalapeño peppers, seeded and thinly sliced
1 small red bell pepper, seeded and thinly sliced
2 baby bok choy, coarsely chopped
4 scallions, thinly sliced
4 portions fresh Hokkien noodles (substitute linguini or vermicelli, prepared according to package directions)

Curry Paste:
Combine all ingredients in a blender or food processor and puree to a fine paste, adding water a little at a time as needed for consistency. Set aside until needed.

Sauce:
Combine all ingredients in a large measuring cup. Whisk to thoroughly mix and set aside until needed.

Stir Fry:
Heat sesame oil in a large wok or skillet. Add shrimp and carrots and stir-fry until shrimp turn pink. Add peppers and bok choy and continue stir-frying until vegetables are nearly tender. Add curry paste and sauce and simmer until slightly thickened. Add scallions and noodles and toss to coat. Remove from heat and divide into serving dishes.

Cook's Note: Any combination of vegetables, meats, or seafood may be used in the stir-fry.

Indonesia

The country and culture known as Indonesia encompasses a vast archipelago in the South Pacific that includes the islands of Bali, Java, Sumatra, and Kalimantan, along with thousands of islets, including the Spice Islands, each with its own unique culinary palette. Seafood and tropical fruits abound, and the cuisine is influenced by centuries of international trade.

As with the cuisines of Malaysia and Singapore, the traditional dishes of Indonesia feature essentially the same array of ingredients. And like that of its neighbors, Indonesian cuisine is highly influenced by Malay, Chinese, Indian, and European cookery. Spice pastes are the heart and soul of many dishes, especially the different varieties of fiery chili *sambal*, which are ubiquitous to Indonesian cuisine.

Indonesian curry encompasses a flavorful array of dishes that includes simple grilled kebabs with spicy peanut sauce, steamed and deep-fried dumplings, stir-fried rice medleys, and rich stews steeped in coconut milk.

For my Indonesian curry menu, I have created my own enticing recipes for Rendang Beef, Tamarind Chicken, Indian Muslim Mee Goring Noodles, and Curry Pork-Filled Sticky Rice in Banana Leaves.

Curry Asia!

Rendang Beef Curry

Serves 4

Curry Paste:
2 stalks lemongrass, peeled and coarsely
  chopped
1 jalapeño pepper, seeded and coarsely
  chopped
4 cloves garlic, coarsely chopped
1 knob gingerroot, peeled and coarsely
  chopped
1 shallot, peeled and coarsely chopped
1 teaspoon cumin
1 teaspoon coriander
1 teaspoon turmeric
1/4 teaspoon cinnamon
1 lime, juice only
1/4 cup water (as needed)

Rendang Beef Curry:
2 tablespoons peanut oil
2 pounds lean beef, cut into 1-inch cubes
1 small onion, peeled and thinly sliced
Curry Paste (see recipe)
1 cup beef stock
1 can unsweetened coconut milk (13.5
  ounces)
2 jalapeño peppers, seeded and thinly sliced
1 small red bell pepper, seeded and coarsely
  chopped
2 limes, cut into wedges

Curry Paste:
Place all ingredients except water in a blender or food processor. Puree mixture to a fine paste, adding water a little at a time as needed for consistency. Set aside until needed.

Rendang Beef Curry:
Heat oil in a large wok over medium heat. Add beef and onions and stir-fry until beef is browned on all sides. Add curry paste and beef stock and stir thoroughly. Reduce heat and simmer uncovered for 30 minutes, stirring frequently. Add coconut milk and continue simmering for 10 minutes, until sauce is thickened and meat is tender. Add peppers and continue simmering for about 5 minutes, until peppers are tender. Serve with steamed rice and lime wedges.

Curry Asia!

Tamarind Chicken

Serves 4

Curry Paste:

4 cloves garlic

1 knob gingerroot, peeled and finely shredded (about 1 tablespoon)

1 stalk lemongrass, bottom half only, trimmed and coarsely chopped

1 shallot, peeled and coarsely chopped

1 teaspoon *sambal oelek* (chili paste)

1 tablespoon tamarind paste

1 teaspoon sesame oil

2 tablespoons sweet soy sauce

1/4 cup water (as needed)

Tamarind Chicken:

2 pounds boneless, skinless chicken breasts or thighs, cut into bite-sized pieces

Curry Paste (see recipe)

1 tablespoon peanut oil

2 jalapeño peppers, seeded and thinly sliced

2 medium tomatoes, cored and coarsely chopped

4 scallions, trimmed and thinly sliced

Curry Paste:

Place all ingredients except water in a blender or food processor. Puree mixture to a fine paste, adding water a little at a time as needed for consistency. Set aside until needed.

Tamarind Chicken:

Combine chicken and curry paste in a large bowl and stir to thoroughly mix. Cover and refrigerate for 1 hour, or overnight. Remove chicken from marinade and reserve remaining marinade for the sauce. Heat oil in a wok. Add chicken, jalapeño, tomatoes and reserved marinade and bring to a simmer. Cover and simmer for 30 minutes, stirring frequently until chicken is tender and sauce is thickened. Stir in scallions and serve with steamed rice.

Mee Goreng

Serves 4

2 tablespoons peanut oil
1 pound boneless chicken breasts or thighs, cut into bite-sized pieces
2 eggs, lightly beaten
4 scallions, thinly sliced
1 jalapeño pepper, seeded and thinly sliced
Curry Paste (see recipe)

1 cup chicken stock
4 portions of *mee goreng* noodles, cooked according to package directions (substitute spaghetti)
2 cups cabbage, finely shredded
2 limes, cut into wedges

Heat oil in a wok, add chicken and stir-fry until lightly browned. Push the chicken pieces to the edge of the wok, pour the beaten eggs into the center of the wok and lightly scramble. Add scallions and jalapeño and stir-fry with the chicken and eggs until tender and fragrant. Stir in curry paste, and chicken stock, Add noodles and cabbage and toss to evenly distribute all ingredients. Immediately transfer to serving dishes and garnish with lime wedges.

Cook's Note: After cooking and draining, noodles may be tossed with a little oil to prevent them from sticking. For spicy noodles, I like to use chili oil.

Curry Asia!

Curry Pork-filled Sticky Rice

Serves 4

Curry Paste:
4 cloves garlic, peeled and minced
1 knob gingerroot, peeled and finely shredded (about 1 tablespoon)
1 teaspoon cumin
1 teaspoon coriander
1/2 teaspoon turmeric
1/4 teaspoon cinnamon
1 teaspoon dried chili flakes (more or less to taste)
1/4 cup water (as needed)

Curry Pork Filling:
1 tablespoon peanut oil
1/2 pound ground pork
1 shallot, peeled and minced
1 jalapeño pepper, seeded and minced
Curry Paste (see recipe)
1 cup coconut milk
1 tablespoon *kekap manis* (sweet soy sauce)
4 cups cooked short grain rice, cooled
12 banana leaf sheets, cut into 8" squares (substitute 8" squares of aluminum foil)

Curry Paste:
Place all ingredients except water in a blender or food processor. Puree mixture to a fine paste, adding water a little at a time as needed for consistency. Set aside until needed.

Curry Pork Filling:
Heat oil in a wok. Stir-fry pork, shallot and jalapeño until meat is lightly browned. Stir in curry paste, add coconut milk and kekap manis. Reduce heat and simmer, stirring frequently, until coconut milk is completely absorbed and evaporated, about 30 minutes. Remove from heat and set aside to cool.

To soften the banana leaves if needed, blanch in boiling water for about 1 minute. Remove leaves from the water, drain, and set aside to cool.

To assemble, using an ice cream scoop or large spoon, place a scoop of rice in the center of each leaf and flatten with the back of the scoop. Place a tablespoon of pork filling in the center of the rice, and top the filling with another tablespoon of rice. Fold the upper and lower edges of the leaf in a pyramid shape around the filling and tuck the ends underneath. Place packets into a steam kettle and steam for about 15 minutes, until rice and filling are heated through. Makes one dozen.

Spotlight on Spice: Sambal

Long before I was bitten by the international food bug, years ago when I knew nothing of Asian food, Gil Pryor, the chef at the St. George Restaurant in the Napa Valley, where I used to work as a waitress and bartender, came back from Tin's Asian Market in Oakland with a jar of *sambal oelek*. He jokingly referred to it as "Hotter Than Seven Bitches" chili sauce, and that evening he used it to make a spicy shrimp dish, a sold-out special that soon became a regular favorite with the St. George patrons.

Of course I'd never heard of sambal oelek, and knew not that it was a staple of Pacific island cuisines. However, I have since come to know that there are many types of *sambal*, which, in one form or another, are the heart and soul of Indonesian food. Sambal may be added to recipes as a flavoring agent, or served as a condiment at the table.

Although the term *Sambal* also refers to an aboriginal group native to the Philippines, sambal is most commonly known as a spicy, chili pepper-based condiment used in the cuisines of Indonesia, Malaysia, Singapore, and Sri Lanka. Types of chili peppers most commonly used are habanero, cayenne, *prik kii nuu* (Thai), *cabe rawit* (Indonesian), *lombok* (Java), and *naga jolokia* (Taliwang).

The various types of sambal include:

Sambal Asam:	chili peppers and tamarind.
Sambal Bajak:	chili peppers, garlic, shrimp paste, and candlenuts.
Sambal Balado:	chili peppers, oil, garlic, onion, tomato, salt and lemon or lime juice.
Sambal Belcan:	shrimp paste, tomatoes, mangoes, sugar and lime juice.
Sambal Tumis:	shrimp paste, onions, garlic, and tamarind.
Sambal Kemiri:	red and green chili peppers, shrimp paste, candlenuts and lime juice.
Sambal Manis:	chili peppers, onions and sugar.
Sambal Trassi:	chili peppers, shrimp paste, sugar, and lemon or lime juice.
Sambal Udang:	chili peppers oil, garlic and shrimp paste.
Sambal Oelek:	chili peppers and lime. The term oelek is the name for a bamboo pestle.
Sambal Udang:	chili peppers, garlic and shrimp paste.
Sambal Jeruk:	green chili peppers and lemon or vinegar.
Sambal Setan:	Madame Jeanette peppers.
Sambal Pedas Pedas:	extra hot chili peppers and lime.
Sambal Taliwang:	extremely spicy naga jolokia peppers, shrimp paste and garlic.

Sambal may be purchased at Asian and international markets, or from online retailers.

The Philippines

The Philippines comprise a nation of more than 7,000 islands in the warm tropical waters of the South Pacific. Filipino culture and its cuisine have been strongly influenced by Spanish, Indonesian, Malaysian, Chinese, and Muslim trading colonies throughout the centuries. As a result, traditional dishes include such ethnically diverse ingredients as Southeast Asian fish sauce, water buffalo cheese, Portuguese chorizo, and Spanish linguica sausages. Seafood is abundant, as are tropical fruit such as coconut, mango and banana.

Although Philippine cuisine features hundreds of delicious dishes, the most common and popular are *adobo*, *empanadas*, *escabeche*, *lumpia*, *kinilaw*, and *pancit*. Adobo, considered the national dish of the Philippines, may be made with chicken or pork, braised in vinegar and spices. Empanadas are meat filled pastries. Lumpia are pancake wraps filled with lettuce leaves and various meats and seafood, with a soy-vinegar dipping sauce. Escabeche is a sweet-and-sour style fish dish. Kinilaw is a ceviche-like seafood dish marinated in lime juice and coconut milk. Pancit is a spicy noodle dish with a variety of meats and vegetables in a savory broth.

Although most of the basic meat, seafood and vegetable elements of Philippine cuisine are quite common, a few specialty ingredients are essential for an authentic rendition in your home kitchen. Among them are tamarind paste or powder, oyster sauce, chili garlic sauce, black bean sauce, shrimp paste, *patis* (fish sauce), palm or rice vinegar, coconut milk, *macapuno* preserves, sesame oil, and soy sauce. Fresh ingredients might include limes, jicama, gingerroot, hearts of palm, chayote, jackfruit, chili peppers, and for the Portuguese effect, chorizo.

Food is a way of life in the Philippines, and with it comes Filipino hospitality. The Filipino people are quick to invite visitors to join them for a meal. If invited, it is considered polite to refuse the first invitation by saying you've already eaten, and wait for a second invitation before accepting.

A Filipino meal is typically served all at once rather than in courses, and is accompanied by a variety of condiments and dipping sauces. A little food left on the plate serves as a signal that one's appetite has been sated. Many Filipino dishes are eaten with the hands, but when silverware is used, it is customary to hold a spoon in one hand and a fork in the other. Knives are usually unnecessary.

A typical day includes three meals, which are often supplemented in between with a second breakfast called *segundo almuerzo*, and an afternoon snack called *merienda*. In the rural areas, lunch is the main meal, whereas in the cities, the evening meal is the most substantial. Seafood, rice, and vegetables are the main staples, and where there is a lack of refrigeration, the primary ingredients are purchased fresh daily, or preserved with salt. Cooking techniques are fresh and simple, with the most common being stir-frying, stewing, and grilling.

Although Philippine curry fits within the general concept of the dish, the interpretation differs somewhat from those of the Asian continent and subcontinent. Philippine curry recipes typically call for curry powder rather than the custom-blended spice palettes I've been using.

As might be expected in this tropical climate, Philippine curry sauces call for coconut milk as the liquid ingredient, with patis (fish sauce) as the main flavoring agent. Seafood and chicken are the most popular main ingredients. Ginger, garlic, and onions are also essential components. However, the fiery chili peppers common to other types of curry are conspicuously absent from Philippine curry recipes. One other notable difference is the addition of garden vegetables such as eggplant, squash, green beans, bell peppers, and potatoes to the stew.

Curry Asia!

Filipino Chicken and Vegetable Curry

Serves 4

1 tablespoon peanut oil
8 chicken drumsticks, skin intact
4 cloves garlic, peeled and minced
1 medium onion, peeled and thinly sliced
1 tablespoon patis (fish sauce)
2 tablespoons mild curry powder
1/2 teaspoon black pepper

2 cups chicken stock
1 red bell pepper, cut into bite-sized pieces
2 stalks celery, thickly sliced
3 red potatoes, cut into bite-sized pieces
1 cup green beans, cut into 1-inch lengths
1 can unsweetened coconut milk (13.5 ounces)

Heat oil in a deep skillet or wok. Add chicken and fry until lightly browned. Add garlic and onions and continue frying until onions are tender. Add patis, and season with curry powder and black pepper. Add water and bring to a simmer. Reduce heat, cover and continue simmering for 20 minutes, turning chicken pieces every 10 minutes. Add bell pepper, celery, potatoes, and green beans. Stir in coconut milk, cover and continue simmering for 20 minutes, stirring occasionally until vegetables are tender. Serve with steamed rice.

Filipino Fish Curry

Serves 4

1 tablespoon peanut oil
1 small onion, peeled and thinly sliced
4 cloves garlic, peeled and minced
1 knob gingerroot, peeled and finely shredded
1 tablespoon patis (fish sauce)
1 tablespoon curry powder
2 jalapeño peppers, seeded and thinly sliced

1 small red bell pepper, seeded and diced
1 cup corn kernels (fresh or frozen)
1 cup green beans, cut into 1-inch lengths
1 can unsweetened coconut milk (13.5 ounces)
4 large, firm white fish filets (tilapia, catfish, snapper, etc.)
2 limes, cut into wedges

Heat oil in a deep skillet or wok. Add onion, garlic, and ginger and stir-fry until onion is translucent. Stir in patis and curry powder. Add peppers, corn, and green beans and continue stir-frying until vegetables are just tender. Stir in coconut milk and bring to a simmer. Add fish fillets, baste with curry sauce and simmer until fish turns opaque. Serve immediately with steamed rice and lime wedges.

The Island Side Dishes

In addition to the main course, Indonesian meals are known for a profusion of side dishes and condiments. Included in this array are recipes for a Tropical Fruit Relish to nibble before the meal, Coconut Cole Slaw as a refreshing salad component, and a savory Indonesian Fried Rice that may be served as an accompaniment for the curry dishes, or as an ingredient to make Dutch Fried-Rice Croquettes.

Curry Asia!

Tropical Fruit Relish with Shrimp Chips

Serves 4

1 large tomato, cored and coarsely chopped
2 avocados, coarsely mashed
1 ripe mango, peeled and coarsely chopped
1 jalapeño pepper, seeded and minced

4 large fresh basil leaves, finely chopped
3 limes, juice only

1 package shrimp chips for dipping

In a mixing bowl, combine the relish ingredients and stir gently to mix. Serve with Shrimp Chips.

Curry Asia!

Coconut Coleslaw

1/2 cup unsweetened coconut milk
1/4 cup rice vinegar
1 lime, juice only

2 tablespoons sugar
1 package cole slaw mix, or 4 cups white cabbage, finely shredded

Combine coconut milk, rice vinegar, lime juice, and sugar in a jar with a tight-fitting lid and shake vigorously to blend. Place shredded cabbage in a large mixing bowl. Add coconut dressing and mix thoroughly to coat. Refrigerate for 1 hour.

Curry Asia!

Indonesian Fried Rice

2 tablespoons vegetable oil
1/2 pound ground meat (beef, pork, or lamb)
1/2 pound small shrimp
1 onion, finely chopped
4 cloves garlic, peeled and minced
2 jalapeño peppers, seeded and finely chopped

4 scallions, thinly sliced
1 teaspoon cumin
1/4 cup sweet soy sauce
6 cups cooked rice
2 eggs, lightly scrambled and chopped 1 cup chicken stock

Heat oil in a large wok. Add ground meat, shrimp, onion, and garlic and stir-fry until shrimp turn pink. Stir in jalapeños, scallions, cumin, and soy sauce. Add rice, eggs and chicken stock and toss to mix. Remove from heat, cover and set aside for a few minutes before serving.

Cook's Note: If you like it spicy, you may add a teaspoon or more of sambal oelek.

Curry Asia!

Dutch Fried-Rice Croquettes

4 cups Indonesian fried rice (see recipe)
2 tablespoons butter
2 tablespoons flour
1/2 cup chicken stock
1 tablespoon sambal oelek
2 tablespoons kecap manis (sweet soy sauce)

2 eggs, lightly beaten
2 cups fine bread crumbs or panko
Vegetable oil for frying

Place fried rice in a large mixing bowl. Melt butter in a saucepan, add flour and stir over medium heat until mixture is thickened and lightly browned. Add stock, *sambal oelek* and *kecap manis* and stir to thicken. Pour over rice, stir to mix, and set aside to cool.

Form the rice into 2" oval patties, dredge each one first in the beaten egg, and then in the bread crumbs and set aside. Heat about 1" of oil in a large wok or skillet over medium heat. Fry croquettes a few at a time in the oil until golden brown on both sides, turning once. Drain on paper towels. Serve with sweet soy sauce for dipping. Makes about two dozen.

Cook's Note: This dish is best when made with leftover fried rice. Make the rice ahead of time and chill it in the refrigerator overnight.

The Far East

Although the Far East is not widely known for its curry, the cuisines of China, Korea, and Japan all have adaptations on the concept. None are what might be deemed "true curry", but they are delicious nonetheless. And each has its own distinctive characteristics that assimilate indigenous ingredients and preparation techniques into the culinary ethos known as curry.

China

Curry found its way into China by the migration of its citizens into Southeast Asia and the Malay Peninsula. The marriage of the Chinese Princess Hang Li Po to the Sultan Mansur Syah of Malacca in 1459 established strong ties between China and Malaysia. The princess brought with her an entourage of several hundred courtiers, and from this alliance a thriving merchant trade system was established.

Several centuries later, during British colonial times, tin was discovered in the Malaysian jungles, which drew thousands of Chinese workers seeking employment in the mines. In 1957, Malaysia declared its independence from England and many Chinese immigrants returned to China, bringing with them the curries of Malaysia. Over time, these exotic dishes were assimilated into the local cuisine and are now ubiquitous on Chinese menus all over the world.

Paradoxically, Chinese curry recipes are few and far between. Most are very basic, calling for garlic, ginger, and generic curry powder for the spices, and chicken broth thickened with flour or cornstarch for the liquid. Chicken, shrimp, or beef are typical main ingredients, along with an assortment of garden-variety vegetables that includes only peas, carrots, onions, and water chestnuts—simple and straightforward.

To represent Chinese curry, I have created two recipes. One is a velvety Shrimp and Vegetable Curry Stir-Fry. The other is for Pork-Filled Curry Dumplings, inspired by the deep-fried treats that one might find at carts and stalls along the streets of Malaysia.

An Insider's Tip for Creating an Asian Recipe

Sometimes my search for an existing recipe yields dismal results, especially when it comes to certain esoteric dishes. So, when I find myself at the end of my online keyword search results with no luck, I often turn to restaurant menus for inspiration. Many, if not most, menus include fairly detailed descriptions of their dishes, and sometimes that information, coupled with a basic knowledge of the cuisine, is enough to create a relatively authentic rendition. I've also discovered that if I use the Google Image tool, I can find photos of the dish,which is sometimes enough of a cue to get me on my way to creating my own version.

Chinese curry is a good example. I've never ordered curry in a Chinese restaurant, and when I looked and looked for an existing recipe as a basis for creating my own version, the most useful recipe I found was for a basic Chinese curry sauce, but not the dish itself. The sauce recipe looked tasty and authentic, but it still didn't tell me how to create a Chinese curry.

For that, I used a keyword search for Chinese restaurants with curry on their menus. And VOILA! Suddenly I had all the inspiration I needed. The best source described their curry as, "Large shrimps with onions, peas, carrots, and water chestnuts, simmered in a spicy hot curry sauce." There was also one that mentioned pineapple chunks in the medley as well.

With that information, plus a Google collage of Chinese curry photos as a jumping-off place, a basic curry sauce recipe, and my knowledge of Chinese cuisine and cooking techniques, I created a relatively authentic rendition of Chinese Curry Shrimp.

Curry Asia!

Chinese-Style Shrimp Curry Stir-Fry

Serves 4

Curry Sauce:
1 tablespoon peanut oil
4 cloves garlic, peeled and minced
1 knob gingerroot, peeled and finely shredded (about 1 tablespoon)
1 small onion, finely chopped
1 tablespoon curry powder (mild or hot)
1/4 teaspoon Chinese five-spice powder
1 tablespoon brown sugar
3 cups chicken stock

Chinese-Style Shrimp Curry:
1 tablespoon peanut oil
1 pound medium shrimp, peeled and deveined, tails intact
2 carrots, peeled and diced
1 small red bell pepper, seeded and diced
1 cup pea pods
1 cup broccoli florets
1 can whole water chestnuts, drained
Chinese curry sauce (see recipe)
1 tablespoon cornstarch dissolved in 1/4 cup water

Curry Sauce:
Heat oil in a wok or skillet. Add garlic, ginger, and onion and stir-fry until onion is translucent. Add curry powder, five-spice powder, and sugar and stir to form a thick paste. Add chicken stock and simmer for about 20 minutes. Remove from the heat and set aside to cool. Transfer sauce to a food processor and puree to a fine consistency. Strain sauce through a sieve into a saucepan and set aside until needed.

Chinese-Style Shrimp Curry:
Heat oil in a wok or large skillet. Add shrimp and vegetables and stir-fry until shrimp are pink and vegetables are tender. Add curry sauce and bring to a simmer. Add cornstarch mixture and continue simmering until sauce is thickened. Remove from heat and serve with steamed rice.

Pork-Filled Curry Dumplings

Serves 4

1 tablespoon peanut oil
1/4 pound ground pork
4 cloves garlic, peeled and minced
1 knob gingerroot, peeled and finely shredded (about1 tablespoon)
4 scallions, trimmed and thinly sliced
1 large carrot, coarsely grated
1 stalk celery with leaves, finely diced
2 teaspoons curry powder

24 small round wonton wrappers
Vegetable oil for frying
Sweet chili sauce for dipping

Heat oil a wok or skillet over medium heat. Add pork, garlic, and ginger and stir-fry until meat begins to brown. Add scallions, carrot and celery and continue stir-frying until vegetables are tender and meat is browned. Stir in curry powder, remove from heat and set aside to cool. Fill each wonton with about a teaspoon of filling, moisten the edges with water, fold the wrapper around the filling and pleat to seal.

Heat about 1 inch of vegetable oil in a wok or frying pan. Add dumplings a few at a time and fry until golden brown, turning once. Do not overcrowd the pan and work quickly to ensure that dumplings don't burn. Remove from oil and drain on paper towels. Serve with sweet chili sauce.

Cook's Note: For more uniform results, a dumpling press may also be used to seal the dumplings.

お好焼と もんじゃ

新宿牛

讃岐 **うどん**

焼たて 自家製 クレー

北海道牧場直送 牛乳ソフトク

自家製 かのや

自家製 かのや

まそば

酪農家の牛乳ソフトクリーム

クレープ プチバリエ

酪農家の 牛乳ソ

Japan

Of all the wonderful dishes in the spectrum of Japanese cuisine, curry is somewhat of an oddity. Curry was first introduced by the British during the Meiji Era, when Japan opened its ports to foreign traders. Its assimilation into Japanese cuisine is largely due to its use as field rations for the military.

Japanese curry sauce is typically served in one of two ways: as gravy for a meat and vegetable stew called *Karē Raisu* (curry rice), or as a sauce for *Katsu-karē*, a breaded, deep-fried pork or chicken cutlet served over steamed white rice.

In Japan, the curry sauce for this dish is usually made with commercially packaged cubes of curry concentrate that are added to boiling water. However, the commercial mix contains MSG, which gives the sauce a deep, rich flavor, but may cause an allergic reaction. If you are not allergic to MSG, the packaged mix offers a more authentic Japanese curry. However, the version provided here is about as close as you can get without adding MSG to the sauce.

Curry Asia!

Katsu-karē

Serves 4

Curry Sauce:
3 cups hearty beef stock
2 tablespoon peanut oil
3 tablespoons flour
2 tablespoon curry powder
1 teaspoon cumin
1/2 teaspoon garlic powder
1/4 teaspoon cinnamon
1/8 teaspoon ground cloves
1 tablespoon soy sauce
1 tablespoon brown sugar

Tonkatsu:
4 boneless pork chops, sliced or pounded 1/2 inch thin
1 egg, lightly beaten
1 cup *panko* (fine Japanese bread crumbs)
Vegetable oil for frying

Curry Sauce:
Bring beef stock to a boil in a saucepan. Reduce heat and simmer uncovered until stock is reduced to 2 cups. Warm the oil in a separate saucepan over medium heat. Add flour and stir constantly until mixture forms a smooth paste, but do not allow to brown. Add reduced beef stock a little at a time, stirring constantly until sauce begins to thicken. Remove from heat and stir in curry powder, cumin, garlic powder, cinnamon, cloves, soy sauce and brown sugar. Return to heat and simmer, stirring constantly until sauce thickens into a rich gravy. Set aside until needed.

Tonkatsu:
Place beaten egg and panko in two shallow bowls. Dredge pork chops in egg, then in panko. Heat about 1/2 inch of cooking oil in a large skillet over medium heat. Do not overheat oil or panko will brown too quickly before the pork gets done all the way through. Fry pork chops until golden brown on both sides, turning occasionally to ensure even browning, about 3 to 5 minutes per side. Drain on paper towels. Transfer pork chops to a cutting board and slice into 1/2 inch strips. Serve with curry sauce over steamed white rice.

Cook's Note: Katsu-karē may be made with boneless chicken breasts prepared according to the same instructions.

Korea

Curry was introduced to Korea by the Japanese military occupation during World War II. Like the Japanese version, Korean curry is typically made with a packaged mix that contains MSG. However, with a little research, I have created my own from-scratch recipe, which calls for beef (a popular main ingredient in Korean cuisine), lots of garden vegetables, and no MSG. I have also included a recipe for my spicy-delicious Curry Chicken Wings.

Korean-Style Beef and Vegetable Curry

Serves 4

Curry Sauce:
3 tablespoons butter
2 tablespoon flour
2 tablespoons curry powder
2 cups beef stock
Salt to taste

Beef and Vegetable Curry
1 tablespoon peanut oil
1 pound lean boneless beef, cut into small
    pieces
4 cloves garlic, peeled and minced
1 small onion, peeled and coarsely chopped
2 cups water
1 large carrot, peeled and diced
1 large potato, peeled and diced
1 stalk celery, thickly sliced
6 mushrooms, thickly sliced
Curry sauce (see recipe)
1/2 cup corn kernels, fresh or frozen
1/2 cup green peas, fresh or frozen
4 portions steamed rice

Curry Sauce:
Melt butter in a wok or skillet. Add flour and stir constantly until the mixture begins to brown. Stir in curry powder, add beef stock and stir until mixture thickens to sauce consistency. Remove from heat and set aside until needed.

Beef and Vegetable Curry
Heat oil in a large wok or a deep skillet. Add beef and stir-fry until beef begins to brown. Add garlic and onion and continue stir-frying until onion is tender and translucent. Add water and bring to a simmer. Reduce heat, cover and continue simmering for about 30 minutes, until beef is tender. Drain liquid from the pan and set aside. Add carrots and potatoes and stir-fry with beef for 3 minutes. Add celery and mushrooms and continue stir-frying for 2 minutes. Add curry sauce, stir in corn and green peas and bring to a simmer. Cover and continue simmering for about 5 minutes, until vegetables are tender. Serve with steamed rice.

Korean Curry Chicken Wings

Serves 4

Marinade:
1 cup milk
4 cloves garlic, peeled and minced
1 knob gingerroot, peeled and shredded
 (about 1 tablespoon)
1 shallot, peeled and minced
2 tablespoons sugar
1 tablespoon curry powder
Salt and pepper to taste

Sweet and Spicy Glaze:
1/3 cup ketchup
1/2 cup sweet chili sauce
1 tablespoon Worcestershire sauce
1/4 cup water
1 tablespoon peanut oil
4 scallions, thinly sliced
1 teaspoon dried chili flakes (more or less
 to taste)

Deep-Fried Chicken Wings:
12 whole chicken wings, cut into segments
3/4 cup flour
1/4 cup cornstarch
2 tablespoons curry powder
Salt and pepper to taste
Vegetable oil for deep-frying
Sweet & Spicy Glaze (see recipe)
2 tablespoons sesame seeds

Marinade:

Combine all ingredients in a large bowl. Add the chicken wings and stir to thoroughly mix. Marinate for at least one hour, or overnight in the refrigerator.

Sweet and Spicy Glaze:

Combine ketchup, chili sauce, Worcestershire sauce and water in a measuring cup and set aside. Heat oil in a wok or skillet. Add scallions and stir-fry until tender. Add sauce mixture, season with chili flakes, and bring to a simmer. Reduce heat and continue simmering until sauce is slightly thickened. Remove from heat, transfer to a large bowl and set aside until needed.

Deep-Fried Chicken Wings:

Drain the marinade from the chicken wings and discard. Combine flour, cornstarch, salt, pepper, and curry powder in a bowl or a plastic food bag, add chicken wings to the flour mixture and toss to thoroughly coat. Heat the oil over medium heat, add chicken wings a few at a time and fry until only lightly browned, turning occasionally to ensure even cooking.

Remove chicken from oil and drain on paper towels. Allow oil to cool and strain through a fine sieve to remove sediment. Reheat oil over medium-high heat. Refry chicken to a crisp golden-brown. Remove from oil and drain on fresh paper towels. Toss chicken wings in spicy glaze and sprinkle with sesame seeds.

Curry Asia!

The Far East Side Dishes

Brussels Sprout Kimchi

Serves 4

16 Brussels sprouts, trimmed and cut lengthwise into quarters

1/2 cup rice vinegar

1 tablespoon sugar

1 tablespoon chili garlic sauce (more or less, to taste)

1 tablespoon *gochujang* (Korean chili sauce) (more or less, to taste)

1 knob gingerroot, peeled and finely shredded (about 1 tablespoon)

2 cloves garlic, peeled and minced

2 scallions, finely sliced

1 tablespoon fish sauce (*nam pla*, *nuoc mam*, or patis)

1 lime, juice only

Blanch Brussels sprouts in a kettle of boiling, salted water until tender, about 5 minutes. Drain, rinse with cold water, and set aside. Combine all ingredients in a mixing bowl and stir thoroughly. Transfer to a large jar with a tight-fitting lid, using a little extra rice vinegar to fill the jar if needed. Refrigerate for 4 hours, or overnight, turning occasionally for even marinating.

Spotlight on Spice: Kimchi

It comes in many forms—and love it or hate it, *kimchi* is the soul of Korean cuisine. The *kimchi*-making process begins with salt curing. Red pepper powder and other flavoring agents such as ginger, garlic, and various vegetables are added, and the kimchi is then fermented in earthenware jars. Each season and region has its own distinctive kimchi.

Tongbaechu kimchi, made with Chinese (napa) cabbage, is the most common variety, and is an important element of every Korean meal. *Nabak*, a spring kimchi, is composed of both cabbage and radishes. *Baek kimchi*, also called white kimchi, does not feature the powdered red pepper used in other varieties, but rather relies on salt as its flavoring and pickling agent. *Oisobagi* is a seasoned cucumber dish. *Dongchimi* is made with salted radishes. *Chonggak kimchi* is made from turnips, heavily seasoned with red pepper. *Bossam kimchi* contains mussels, pears, dates, and chestnuts wrapped in cabbage leaves. *Kkakdugi* is a diced and peppered white radish kimchi.

Curry Asia!

Japanese Cabbage Slaw

Dressing:
1/4 cup mayonnaise
1/4 cup Kewpie mayonnaise (spicy)
1/4 cup rice vinegar
1 tablespoon soy sauce
1 tablespoon sugar

Salad:
1 small head of white cabbage, finely
   shredded (about 4 cups)
1 large carrot, coarsely grated

Dressing:

Combine all ingredients in a measuring cup and set aside until needed.

Salad:

Place cabbage and carrots in a large mixing bowl. Drizzle with dressing and toss to thoroughly mix. Cover and refrigerate until serving time.

Cook's Note: Packaged cole slaw mix may be used for this recipe. However, do not use a mix that contains red cabbage because it will turn the dressing pink!

Resources

Cooking Utensils:

To make the recipes in this cookbook, you will need both everyday cookware, as well as a few special cooking utensils. Your everyday cookware should include sauté pans, saucepans, and lids in several sizes; a large skillet with a lid; and a large soup kettle with a lid. Your basic cookware should also include covered baking dishes in several sizes, baking sheets in several sizes, a large roasting pan, a steamer basket, and a set of wire racks. A cast-iron grill pan/griddle is also an excellent cooking device.

Measuring cups and spoons, mixing bowls, a colander, and a set of storage containers are essential. You will also need a set of sharp knives in several sizes, a sharpening steel, and cutting boards in several sizes, plus an extra large board for rolling dough.

Gadgets and small utensils should include a vegetable peeler, a box grater, spoons and spatulas in several sizes (both wooden and stainless steel), a ladle, a pair of tongs, a whisk, a strainer, a rolling pin, a can opener, a basting brush, and a pair of kitchen scissors. Two special items for preparing Asian food are a mandolin for fine slicing, and a fine shredder for preparing ginger.

Certain electrical appliances not only offer time-saving convenience, some of them may also produce better results than the same tasks done by hand. Those appliances include a microwave, a rice cooker, a blender or food processor (I have both), and an electric wok with a thermostat. For curry powders, an electric coffee mill is indispensible for grinding spices to a fine powder.

When it comes to cooking pans, it goes without saying that the one essential for Asian cuisine is a good wok. I have two: a traditional cast iron model, and a non-stick model. Both have their appeal. The cast-iron model is excellent for steaming and deep-frying, while the non-stick model works well for stir-frying and is easy to clean and maintain.

I also have a special curry pan manufactured by T-Fal, which I purchased solely for Curry Asia! It's ten inches wide and four inches deep, with a standard straight handle, plus an extra loop handle on the opposite side. It has a marvelous non-stick surface, and a domed glass lid. At $29.99, it is one of the best cookware purchases I've ever made.

An outdoor barbeque is also a welcome amenity, since a charcoal grill yields the best flavor. But an electric countertop grill or a stovetop grill pan will also suffice.

Curry Spices:

Cayenne pepper
Chili powder
Coriander seeds
Cumin seeds
Fennel Seeds
Fenugreek
Garam masala
Garlic powder
Ground Cinnamon
Ground Coriander
Ground Cumin
Ground Ginger
Ground Mustard
Ground Turmeric
Mustard seeds
Nigella (Onion Seeds)
Paprika
Whole Black peppercorns
Whole Cinnamon
Whole Cloves
Whole Nutmeg

Spotlight on Spice: Curry Powder

The term *curry* is not synonymous with curry powder. Curry is actually a classification of cooking techniques for any of a number of meat and vegetable dishes flavored with an array of spices. Curry powder is a general term for the various spice blends that are often used to flavor curries. However, not all curries contain curry powder, and although the word curry may be strongly associated with Indian cuisine, curry is not unique to India. Many Asian cuisines feature their own unique styles of curry, including those of Sri Lanka, Indonesia, Malaysia, and Thailand, all of which are flavored with their own traditional spice blends.

First introduced to the English language during the British colonial era in India, the word 'curry' is an anglicized pronunciation of the Tamil word *kari* (also *karhi* and *curriel*), a thick, spicy sauce. While each region of India has its own style and spice, since the introduction of curry powder to the West, the flavor of most commercially prepared curry powders has become rather standardized, and are generally available in two styles, regular, and spicy Madras.

A commercial curry powder may contain twenty or more spices, including black pepper, cardamom, cinnamon, cloves, coriander, cumin, fennel seed, fenugreek, ginger, garlic, mace, mustard seeds, nutmeg, poppy seeds, red pepper, saffron, sesame seeds, tamarind, and turmeric, which gives curry powder its ruddy yellow color.

In India, curry powders from southern regions tend to be spicy, while those from the northern regions are milder. When the individual spices are freshly ground, their flavors are more pungent. Some curry powders also feature toasted spices, which brings out deeper flavors.

Another Indian spice blend is *garam masala*, which means hot spice paste or blend. These blends tend to include spices that are characteristically 'warm' in flavor and aroma, and are usually added at the end of the cooking process to preserve their pungency.

Garam masala is similar to curry powder, but with a more specific set of ingredients. Although it varies according to region and individual cooks, a common garam masala blend includes cinnamon, cloves, cardamom, nutmeg, and black pepper. Other ingredients may include black or white peppercorns, bay leaves, coriander, cumin, long pepper, mace, nutmeg, and star anise.

Basic Curry Powder Recipe

1/3 cup cumin
1/4 cup coriander
1/4 cup turmeric
2 tablespoons cinnamon
1 teaspoon cayenne pepper
1 tablespoon chili powder
1 tablespoon paprika
1 tablespoon garlic powder

Combine all spices in a large measuring cup or bowl and stir to thoroughly blend. Store in an airtight container.

Stock Recipes

A high-quality stock is an important foundation for any sauce or soup. There are many good commercially packaged stocks available, but I still prefer to make my own because it allows me to control additives such as salt, MSG, and preservatives. It's also an excellent way for me to reduce kitchen waste by using up meat scraps, bones, and vegetable trimmings.

Beef Stock

2 pounds beef bones
2 tablespoons vegetable oil
2 carrots, coarsely chopped
1 onion, coarsely chopped
2 stalks celery, coarsely chopped
1 small piece leek, chopped and thoroughly rinsed (about 1/2 cup)
3 cloves garlic, crushed
12 cups water
2 bay leaves
Salt and pepper to taste

Preheat oven to 400 degrees and roast beef bones for 1 hour. Heat the oil in a large kettle. Add carrots, onion, celery, leek, and garlic. Reduce heat to low and allow vegetables to sweat, stirring occasionally until tender and translucent, about 10 minutes. Add water, roasted beef bones, and bay leaves. Bring to a boil, reduce heat, and simmer on very low heat for about 2 hours, until broth is reduced by about half. Remove from heat and set aside to cool. Strain the stock through a fine sieve. Refrigerate and skim fat before using.

Chicken Stock

2 pounds chicken bones (or backs and wings)
2 tablespoons vegetable oil
12 cups water
2 carrots, coarsely chopped
1 onion, coarsely chopped
2 stalks celery, coarsely chopped
1 small piece leek, chopped and thoroughly rinsed (about 1/2 cup)
3 cloves garlic, crushed
2 bay leaves
Salt and pepper to taste
Heat the oil in a large kettle, add chicken pieces, and sauté until browned. Add carrots, onion, celery, leek, and garlic, reduce heat to low and allow vegetables to sweat, stirring occasionally until tender and translucent, about 10 minutes. Add water and bay leaves. Bring to a boil, reduce heat, and simmer on very low heat for about 2 hours, until broth is reduced by about half. Remove from heat and set aside to cool. Strain the stock through a fine sieve. Refrigerate and skim fat before using.

Pork Supreme Broth

2 pounds pork neck bones
1 pound chicken bones (or backs and wings)
12 cups water
Salt and pepper to taste

Combine all ingredients in a large soup kettle. Bring to a boil, reduce heat to lowest temperature, and simmer for about 4 hours, until broth is reduced by half. Remove from heat, and set aside to cool. Strain through a fine sieve. Refrigerate and skim off the fat before using.

Vegetable Stock

2 tablespoons vegetable oil
12 cups water
2 carrots, coarsely chopped
1 onion, coarsely chopped
2 stalks celery, coarsely chopped
1 small piece leek, chopped and thoroughly rinsed (about 1/2 cup)
3 cloves garlic, crushed
2 bay leaves
Salt and pepper to taste

Heat oil in a large kettle. Add carrots, onion, celery, leek, and garlic. Reduce heat to low and allow vegetables to sweat, stirring occasionally until tender and translucent, about 10 minutes. Add water and bay leaves, bring to a boil, reduce heat, and simmer on very low heat for about 2 hours, until broth is reduced by about half. Remove from heat and set aside to cool. Strain the stock through a fine sieve. Refrigerate and skim fat before using.

THINGSASIAN PRESS

Experience Asia Through the Eyes of Travelers

"To know the road ahead, ask those coming back."
(CHINESE PROVERB)

East meets West at ThingsAsian Press, where the secrets of
Asia are revealed by the travelers who know them best. Writers
who have lived and worked in Asia. Writers with stories to tell
about basking on the beaches of Thailand, teaching English
conversation in the exclusive salons of Tokyo, trekking in
Bhutan, haggling with antique vendors in the back alleys of
Shanghai, eating spicy noodles on the streets of Jakarta,
photographing the children of Nepal, cycling the length of
Vietnam's Highway One, traveling through Laos on the mighty
Mekong, and falling in love on the island of Kyushu.

Inspired by the many expert, adventurous and independent
contributors who helped us build **ThingsAsian.com**, our
publications are intended for both active travelers and those
who journey vicariously, on the wings of words.

ThingsAsian Press specializes in travel stories, photo journals,
cultural anthologies, destination guides and children's books.
We are dedicated to assisting readers in exploring the cultures
of Asia through the eyes of experienced travelers.

www.thingsasianpress.com